Britain and Empire, 1880–1945

SEMINAR STUDIES IN HISTORY

Britain and Empire, 1880–1945

DANE KENNEDY

Longman

An imprint of **Pearson Education**

London • New York • Toronto • Sydney • Tokyo • Singapore • Hong Kong • Cape Town
New Delhi • Madrid • Paris • Amsterdam • Munich • Milan • Stockholm

PEARSON EDUCATION LIMITED

Head Office:
Edinburgh Gate
Harlow
Essex CM20 2JE
Tel: +44 (0)1279 623623
Fax +44 (0)1279 431059

London Office:
128 Long Acre
London WC2E 9AN
Tel: +44 (0)20 7447 2000
Fax: +44 (0)20 7240 5771
Website: www.history-minds.com

First published in Great Britain in 2002

ISBN 0 582 41493 8

British Library Cataloguing in Publication Data
A CIP catalogue record for this book can be obtained from the British Library

Library of Congress Cataloging in Publication Data
A CIP catalog record for this book can be obtained from the Library of Congress

10 9 8 7 6 5 4 3 2 1

Typeset by 7 in 10/12 Sabon Roman
Printed in Malaysia, LSP

The Publishers' policy is to use paper manufactured from sustainable forests.

For Alene, as she embarks on her university education

CONTENTS

INTRODUCTION TO THE SERIES

Such is the pace of historical enquiry in the modern world that there is an ever-widening gap between the specialist article or monograph, incorporating the results of current research, and general surveys, which inevitably become out of date. *Seminar Studies in History* is designed to bridge this gap. The series was founded by Patrick Richardson in 1966 and his aim was to cover major themes in British, European and World history. Between 1980 and 1996 Roger Lockyer continued his work, before handing the editorship over to Clive Emsley and Gordon Martel. Clive Emsley is Professor of History at the Open University, while Gordon Martel is Professor of International History at the University of Northern British Columbia, Canada, and Senior Research Fellow at De Montfort University.

All the books are written by experts in their field who are not only familiar with the latest research but have often contributed to it. They are frequently revised, in order to take account of new information and interpretations. They provide a selection of documents to illustrate major themes and provoke discussion, and also a guide to further reading. The aim of *Seminar Studies in History* is to clarify complex issues without over-simplifying them, and to stimulate readers into deepening their knowledge and understanding of major themes and topics.

ACKNOWLEDGEMENT

We are grateful to A. P. Watt Limited on behalf of The National Trust for Places of Historical Interest or Natural Beauty for permission to reproduce the poem "Tommy" by Rudyard Kipling.

CHRONOLOGY

1881	Afrikaners defeat British forces at the battle of Majuba Hill in South Africa
1882	British occupy Egypt
1883	Boy's Brigade founded
	Primrose League established
1884	New Guinea divided by Britain and Germany
1885	Death of General Gordon in Sudan
1886	Irish Home Rule proposed by Gladstone, splitting the Liberal Party
	Discovery of gold in the Transvaal, South Africa
1887	First Imperial Conference of dominion leaders convenes in London
	Imperial Institute founded
1889	British South Africa Company granted charter over Southern Rhodesia
1894	Navy League established
1895	Jameson Raid fails to overthrow Transvaal government
1896–97	Ndebele–Shona rebellion in Southern Rhodesia
1899	South African War begins
	Sudan conquered by General Kitchener
1900	Pan-African Congress meets in London
1901	National Service League established
	Victoria League founded
	Commonwealth of Australia created
1902	South African War ends
	Anglo-Japanese Alliance
	Committee of Imperial Defence created
	Trans-Pacific cable joins Britain, Canada, Australia and New Zealand
1903	Joseph Chamberlain launches tariff reform campaign
1904	Anglo-French entente
	Physical Deterioration Committee appointed by Parliament
1907	Anglo-Russian treaty
	Boy Scouts founded by Baden-Powell

1909	Morley–Minto reforms instituted in India
1910	Union of South Africa
	Round Table movement established to promote imperial cause
1911	Coronation Durbar for George V in India
1914	First World War begins
1915	Gallipoli campaign
1916	Easter Rising in Ireland
	Lloyd George coalition government formed
	Empire Day granted official status by Parliament
	Sykes–Picot agreement to partition the Ottoman Empire
1917	Balfour Declaration promises Jewish homeland in Palestine
	Imperial War Cabinet established
1918	First World War ends
	Reform Act enfranchises all males over the age of 21 and most females over the age of 30
1919	Amritsar massacre in India
	Rowlatt Acts suppress political agitation in India
	Government of India Act introduces dyarchy
	Sinn Fein launches war for Irish independence
	Overseas Settlement Committee created
	Race riots in British port cities
	Alien Restriction Act empowers government to deport aliens
1920	Britain receives mandates over Iraq and Palestine
1921	Washington Naval Conference
	Anglo-Irish Treaty establishes Irish Free State
	Gandhi launches first civil disobedience campaign
1922	Chanak Crisis
	Empire Settlement Act
	Lloyd George coalition government collapses
1923	White Paper declares 'paramountcy' of African interests in Kenya
1924	British Empire Exhibition opens at Wembley
1925	Dominions Office created
	Special Restriction (Coloured Alien Seamen) Order
1926	General Strike in Britain
	Balfour Report proposes Commonwealth definition
	Empire Marketing Board established
1927	Simon Commission investigates Indian constitutional reform
1929	Colonial Development Act

1930	Statute of Westminster creates British Commonwealth
	First Round Table Conference on India's political future
	Gandhi launches second civil disobedience campaign
1931	National Government established
1932	Ottawa Conference institutes imperial preference
	King's first Christmas Day speech broadcast to empire
1935	Government of India Act creates provincial self-government
	Italy invades Ethiopia
1937	Japan launches war against China
1938	Germany annexes Austria, threatens Czechoslovakia; Munich agreement
	Naval base at Singapore completed
1939	Second World War begins
1940	Colonial Development and Welfare Act
1941	Britain and the United States draft the Atlantic Charter
	Japan enters the Second World War
1942	Singapore, Malaya and Burma fall to the Japanese
	Cripps mission to placate Indian nationalists fails
	Congress launches the 'Quit India' campaign
	Beveridge Report recommends post-war welfare state
1945	Colonial Development and Welfare Act
	Second World War ends

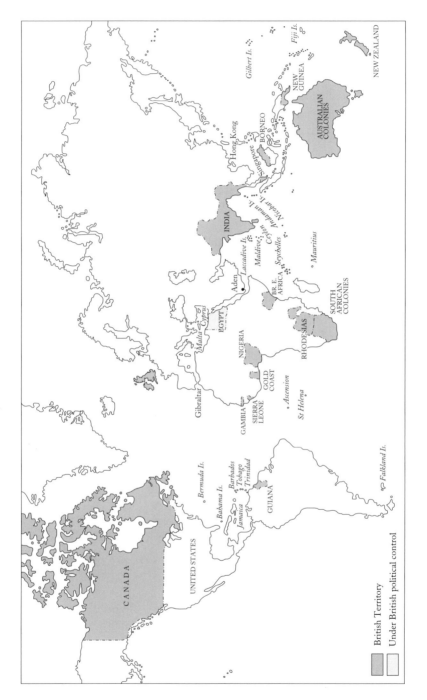

Map 1   The British Empire in 1897

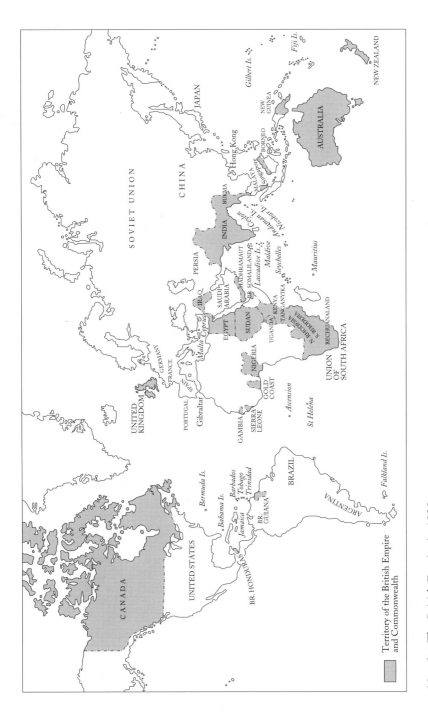

Map 2   The British Empire in 1920

Territory of the British Empire and Commonwealth

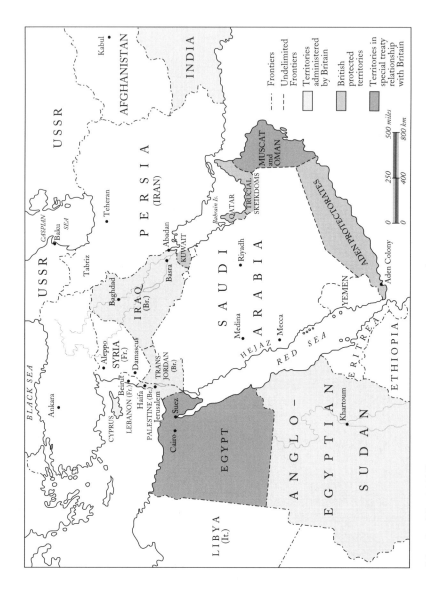

Map 3 The Middle East in 1926

PART ONE INTRODUCTION

CHAPTER ONE

BACKGROUND AND CONTEXT

Perhaps the most paradoxical feature of modern British history is that the British Empire reached its zenith as British economic and military power went into retreat. Starting with the scramble for Africa in the late nineteenth century, those parts of the map painted a British red spread at an unprecedented rate, culminating in the great tracts of Middle Eastern and African territory claimed as the spoils of the First World War. Despite some concessions to subject peoples, the British retained their vast empire to the outbreak of the Second World War, and, excepting the East Asian territories captured by Japan, through to its conclusion. Over this same period, however, Britain's economic and military might experienced a distinct decline relative to other powers. Its mid-nineteenth-century pre-eminence as 'the workshop of the world' came under challenge in the closing decades of the century from newly industrialised countries like Germany and the United States of America and the naval power that underwrote its trading supremacy was likewise undermined by these rivals. The First World War's devastating drain of resources left Britain seriously weakened, and the global conflict that broke out in 1939 furthered its contraction to a second-tier power.

How can we reconcile these seemingly contradictory developments? How was it possible for Britain to extend its empire and enforce its authority over hundreds of millions of peoples at the same time that its economic and political claims to world power were becoming increasingly fragile? In wrestling with these questions, it is helpful to glance backwards over the course of Britain's imperial experience with an eye to broad patterns. The greatest burst of expansion prior to the late nineteenth century occurred in the long eighteenth century, as the newly established United Kingdom (incorporating England, Scotland, Wales, and eventually Ireland into a single British state) undertook a series of wars against its European rivals, including the Dutch, the Spanish, and especially the French. By the time the last of these wars came to a close on the battlefield of Waterloo, Britain possessed an empire that extended across the world's oceans, binding Canada, the Caribbean, South Africa, India, Australia, and innumerable other lands to a London-based political and economic system. With no serious challengers to their global position after 1815, the British felt far less compulsion to lay claim to further overseas territory. Their interests were often enough served through the independent enterprise of manufacturers, merchants and bankers, whose success in dominating international markets was evidence of the triumph of the new industrial capitalism that was reshaping Britain itself. The result was the growth of what historians have termed the 'informal empire', extending to decaying old dynasties like Qing China and the Ottoman Empire and unstable new countries like the Latin American republics. These states, while retaining some semblance of political autonomy, lacked the strength to resist Britain's economic encroachments: when they tried, the British government was quite prepared to employ 'gunboat diplomacy' to protect the interests of its traders. The formal empire did, to be sure, continue to expand in the early and mid-Victorian years, but it did so in a fitful manner that was driven more often by pressures on the colonial frontier than by policies in the imperial metropolis. Within Britain, the dominant response was disinterest, while an active hostility to empire, rooted in the liberal conviction that it encouraged authoritarian, protectionist policies, was as prevalent as any imperial enthusiasm. Thus, the empire's return to a prominent place in the preoccupations of Britain's policy makers and the consciousness of its public towards the end of the nineteenth century marked a significant departure from the trends that had dominated the preceding era.

What this brief overview suggests is that the most aggressively expansionist periods in British history occurred when British power confronted serious challenges from rival states, not when it stood supreme in world affairs. Unable to rely on informal influence in the face of competition, the British sought to bolster their uncertain international position through exclusive claims to colonial territory. These efforts eventuated in triumph at the end of the long eighteenth century; the new era of imperialism that began around 1880 brought a very different outcome. The exponents of empire, however, were by no means aware that their cause would end as it did, and we would do well to resist the temptations of hindsight, with its tincture of inevitability.

When Britain entered the era of heightened imperial activity that extended from the scramble for Africa through to the Second World War, the course it charted was influenced by a variety of currents, many of them rapidly changing and highly unpredictable. The international environment that had favoured British interests in the middle decades of the nineteenth century was profoundly altered towards its end by the growing political power of two traditional rivals, France and Russia, and two new challengers, the United States and Germany. The latter state, in particular, complicated the diplomatic calculus for Britain, but all presented new or intensified threats to its strategic position around the globe. Moreover, the rapid industrialisation of Germany, the United States and France made their economies increasingly fierce competitors in markets that British manufacturers had comfortably claimed as their own earlier in the century: even Lilliputian Belgium established a steel industry that set Birmingham on its heels. It was agriculture, however, that was the first to feel the full brunt of competition. The global spread of cheap and reliable railway and shipping systems allowed North American grain, Argentine beef, New Zealand butter, and various other agricultural goods to flood the British market, causing commodity prices and land values to plummet. The trade slump that began in 1873 and continued with a few brief interruptions for the next twenty years seemed to many Britons a harbinger of things to come. Empire, or more particularly a politically and economically integrated imperial system that promised shelter from such unwelcome international trends, was regarded with renewed interest.

Britain's turn to a more consciously imperialist course was also shaped by a number of domestic developments. Doubtless the most momentous was the transition to democratic politics. The enfranchisement of most urban working-class males in 1867, followed by their rural counterparts in 1884, transformed the nature of British politics towards the end of the century. Although William Gladstone is credited with making the first direct appeal to a mass electorate, his political opponents soon learned that they could mobilise popular support by fostering nationalist pride, which was invariably associated with the assertion of British power abroad, particularly when it inspired individual acts of heroism in colonial campaigns. Underwriting the rise of the new imperial politics were the public rituals of a resurgent monarchy, the jingoistic enthusiasms of the popular press and the music halls, and the racialist attitudes that percolated up from various sources. Social Darwinism soon supplied a scientifically sanctioned doctrine that legitimated the imperialist world-view, with its implicit understanding of the international scene as an unforgiving struggle for survival that pitted nation against nation, race against race. It also posed disturbing questions about whether the British were prepared for this struggle and proposed sweeping measures to make them so. An important consequence of these varied developments would be the radical transformation of the role of government in the social and economic life of its citizens, a transformation that has been characterised by some historians as the creation of a social imperial state. While social imperialism's agenda was never fully realised, it made sufficient inroads to substantiate the importance of empire within Britain itself.

The purpose of this volume, then, is to trace the relationship between Britain and its empire in the period when the two were bound together in an intimate embrace. By writing what in effect is an *imperial* history of Britain, I am drawing on insights and inspiration from a growing array of scholars who have sought to show how integral the empire was to the British experience. The past half dozen years or so have brought an especially abundant harvest of research offering empirical evidence of and theoretical perspectives on the connections between Britain and its empire (e.g., Burton, 1994, 1998; Bush, 1999; Cannadine, 2001; Lahiri, 2000; Parsons, 1998; Schneer, 1999; Tabili, 1994; Thompson, 2000). For all their claims to originality, however, these studies follow in the wake of several earlier waves of enquiry that made important advances in our under-standing of imperial Britain, most notably the valuable work published in the 1960s on British imperial ideology (e.g., Koebner and Schmidt, 1964; Porter, 1968; Semmel, 1968; Thornton, 1968) and the influential studies of imperialism and popular culture by John MacKenzie and others in the 1980s (e.g., August, 1985; MacKenzie, 1984, 1986; Mangan, 1986; Rich, 1986; Rosenthal, 1986). Nor can we neglect the information and insights to be garnered from the two historiographical traditions that the preceding scholarship has sought to bridge and transcend – an imperial one that has concerned itself mainly with Britain's impact on its overseas possessions and a national one that has concerned itself mainly with Britain's internal social and political developments. The purpose of this volume is to provide a brief and suggestive synthesis that signals some of the themes this rich and varied literature has shown shaped Britain at the height of empire.

PART TWO   ANALYSIS

CHAPTER TWO

IMPERIAL EXPANSION AND NATIONAL FOREBODING, 1880–1900

For the British people and their leaders, imperialism acquired a new importance – and a new meaning – in the late nineteenth century. Hitherto associated in the minds of most Victorians with the military adventurism of continental despots like Napoleon, the term took on more positive connotations in public discourse as various forces combined to cause the British to rethink who they were and where they stood in the world (Koebner and Schmidt, 1964). These forces ranged from the foreign economic and military threats posed by aggressive rivals like the newly industrialised United States and the newly unified Germany to the domestic political and social demands made by subordinate groups like newly enfranchised working-class men and newly assertive middle-class women. All of them were set in a context that construed imperialism as an enterprise that could check their potentially destabilising effects or divert them into more beneficial channels. Although the British Empire already existed as a global system, during this period it expanded at an unmatched speed, incorporating large tracts of territory in Africa, Asia and the Pacific, and it assumed an unprecedented place in the national consciousness, altering the very meaning of what it meant to be British. In consequence, the boundaries between the international and the domestic spheres – or, more precisely, between empire and nation – began to blur.

THE POLITICS OF IMPERIALISM

The fall of the Conservative government in 1880 appeared to many a repudiation of Benjamin Disraeli's forward foreign policy, with its appeal to national pride and assertion of imperial power. Certainly the Liberal leader, William Gladstone, thought so. His acclaimed Midlothian campaigns of 1879–80 mobilised public opinion in opposition to Disraeli's handling of the 'Eastern Question', which had placed Britain's strategic interest in maintaining an Ottoman buffer against Russian expansion above the nation's moral revulsion at the Ottoman massacre of Bulgarian Christians.

Combined with the political embarrassment caused by setbacks in 1879 in Afghanistan, where a popular uprising forced a British occupying army into retreat, and Zululand in South Africa, where British forces were cut to pieces at the battle of Isandlwana, the public rejection of Disraeli's Balkan strategy seemed to demonstrate the unpopularity of a foreign policy framed around the naked self-interests of the state. Gladstone came to office determined to reassert Britain's claims to be a moral force in world affairs. Although this ambition carried more assertive implications than critics allowed when they charged Gladstone with isolationist or 'Little Englander' impulses, he *was* in principle antagonistic to any further additions to the imperial portfolio and eager to divest the nation of those recent acquisitions that he viewed as unwise and unethical investments (Shannon, 1976).

It is a measure of the sea-change in both the international and the domestic climate after 1880 that Gladstone so soon found himself obliged to abandon the precepts of his liberal conscience. The crisis came in Egypt, where the Khedive had spent his country into bankruptcy and dependency on Britain and France. When anti-Western nationalists overthrew him in 1882, the security of the Suez Canal and the interests of British investors (including Gladstone, whose portfolio was heavily laden with Egyptian stocks) seemed in jeopardy. Gladstone dispatched troops to restore the Khedive to power, but his action only underlined the point that this deposed and discredited ruler had become the puppet of the British, who found that if they wanted a government to safeguard their interests they would have to provide it themselves. Though the British were officially reluctant to acknowledge the fact, Egypt was entered into the imperial ledger (Robinson and Gallagher, 1968).

When Gladstone did swim against the tide of empire, he found it tough going. In South Africa, his decision to rescind the Conservative government's annexation of the Transvaal came only after its Afrikaner burghers bloodied British troops at the battle of Majuba Hill in 1881, making the reversal in policy look suspiciously like surrender in the eyes of the public. He also ordered the evacuation of British-officered Egyptian garrisons from the Sudan, but failed to reckon with the messianic General Charles 'Chinese' Gordon, who dug in his heels at Khartoum, where he was soon besieged by Sudanese insurgents inspired by their own messianic leader, a Mahdi (Islamic prophet). Press coverage fanned public concern for Gordon's fate, forcing Gladstone to send out a relief force to save him. It arrived too late: Gordon entered the pantheon of martyrs to the imperial cause, while Gladstone became its goat. Neither the withdrawal from the Sudan nor from the Transvaal would stick: by the end of the century, the British had reasserted their claims to both territories.

But the heaviest political price that Gladstone paid for his ambivalence about empire came in Ireland. Motivated in part by his need for the political support of Charles Stewart Parnell's Irish Nationalist Party, but also by his growing conviction that the Irish problem was too deep-seated to be resolved any other way, Gladstone proposed home rule for Ireland in 1886. Ireland was not in any formal sense an imperial dependency: it had sent parliamentary representatives to Westminster since the 1801 Act of Union (though Catholics could not vote until 1829). But its standing in the United Kingdom had long been a subordinate one, as was evident from the economic power enjoyed by absentee landlords, the political power invested in the colonial-style Viceroy and, above all, the military power manifested in the huge number of troops garrisoned on the island. The troubled history of Ireland in the nineteenth century suggests that the Irish never reconciled themselves to their place in the United Kingdom in the manner exhibited by the Scots and the Welsh. Nor did the English show any sign of reconciling themselves to the Irish, at least if widespread representations of the latter as simian-like beasts are accurate measures of popular attitudes (Curtis, 1968). The reaction to Gladstone's Home Rule bill seemed to confirm Ireland's quasi-colonial status. The Conservatives were fiercely opposed, but in many respects the most damaging response came from within the Liberal Party itself. Joseph Chamberlain, one of the Liberals' brightest lights, bolted from the Cabinet and the party, leading a rump group into secession as Liberal Unionists. Chamberlain's quixotic career would take an increasingly imperial trajectory; Ireland was his launching pad (Boyce, 1996).

What makes Gladstone's troubled ministry so instructive is that so many of its troubles arose out of its determination to tack against the wind of imperialism. When it ran aground on the rocks of Irish home rule, some of those left clinging to the wreckage began to reappraise the premises of their political creed. Liberalism seemed to them in sore need of reform, and although they remained adamant in their defence of free trade, they advocated a more active state than acknowledged by their Gladstonian heritage, a state that pursued social reforms at home and national interests abroad. In effect, they sought to accommodate themselves to the new imperial dispensation, as was evident by calling themselves Liberal Imperialists (Matthew, 1973).

The direct consequence of the Liberal débâcle, however, was the return to power of the Conservatives, who were less afflicted than their rivals by doubts and disagreements about the assertion of power abroad. They would hold office for all but three years over the next two decades, a period that saw the empire expand at an unprecedented rate. Though Lord Salisbury and his Conservative colleagues may have been more preoccupied with protecting what they had rather than pushing for more – they were 'reluctant imperialists' in the words of one historian (Lowe, 1967) – they were responsible nonetheless for one of the most remarkable periods of imperial expansion in Britain's history.

THE SCRAMBLE FOR COLONIES

The bare facts of Britain's imperial march across the globe in the late nineteenth century encourage a deceptively simple view of events, analogous to a championship chess match between the British grand master and its brash European challengers. Nationalist rivalries certainly played an important part in the drive to acquire colonial territory, but motives were much messier and more varied than a political-diplomatic perspective alone can reveal. Strategic, economic, and other considerations were so closely intertwined that it is almost impossible to separate them, and perhaps historically misleading to try to do so. The occupation of Egypt is the classic example: the British appear to have intervened to protect both the interests of bondholders and the security of the Suez Canal, which was in turn significant as a strategic *and* a commercial conduit to India and the rest of Asia. None of these considerations would have compelled intervention, of course, if domestic discontent had not caused the collapse of the Khedive's pro-Western regime, leading some historians to suggest that events on the colonial 'periphery' reveal more about the causes of conquest than do the designs of metropolitan statesmen (Robinson and Gallagher, 1968). It is equally evident, however, that regimes like Egypt's became destabilised because of the corrosive effects of Western economic interests, which returns us at another level to a Euro-centred understanding of expansionist forces (Cain and Hopkins, 1993).

The 'scramble for Africa' was the most dramatic manifestation of the late-Victorian burst of imperial expansion. Though it has been suggested that the occupation of Egypt in 1882 provoked a continental-wide scramble for colonial possessions (Robinson and Gallagher, 1968), most of the evidence indicates that the immediate causes varied from region to region (Chamberlain, 1974; Wesseling, 1996). In West Africa, for example, French, German and Dutch advances in the region appear to have persuaded the British that their traders could be cut off from producers and markets in the interior unless they asserted formal claims to territory (Hynes, 1979). These claims included the Oil Rivers Protectorate (1885), which encompassed Southern Nigeria (to which the north would be added in 1900); the Northern Territories Protectorate (1886), a precursor to the Gold Coast (Ghana); and the Sierra Leone Protectorate (1886), incorporating the hinterland to the earlier colonial settlement at Freetown.

In southern and central Africa, a complex array of factors shaped British policy. German claims to South-West Africa (Namibia) helped to provoke the declaration of a British protectorate in neighbouring Bechuanaland (Botswana) in 1885. But the push north also was driven by a determination to contain the Afrikaners of the Transvaal. When the discovery of gold in the heart of the Transvaal in 1886 strengthened the

Afrikaners' economic and political position, this policy took on added importance. So did the suspicion that the fabled 'King Solomon's Mines' were to be found in the lands north of the Limpopo River (Kennedy, 1987). The result was the establishment of protectorates in 1889, 1891 and 1893 over the territories soon to be known as Southern Rhodesia (Zimbabwe), Northern Rhodesia (Zambia) and Nyasaland (Malawi).

The British push into East Africa had its own dynamic. Certainly German activity in the region convinced the British to claim their own sphere of influence, but there was little evidence of economic or strategic gain from the declaration of the East African Protectorate (1886), which encompassed Kenya and Uganda, or the protectorate over Zanzibar (1890). Only later did Salisbury suggest that East Africa's importance was tied to the headwaters of the Nile, which the overwrought *fin-de-siècle* fears of the imperialists imagined to be at risk of diversion by an enemy power eager to wreak havoc on the Egyptian economy. So as to prevent this unlikely outcome – and to revenge the death of Gordon, however belatedly – the British dispatched an army under General Kitchener to conquer the Sudan in 1896, supplying one of the final jingoistic flourishes to the British scramble for African colonies.

Although Africa's size and suspected riches made it the main victim of late nineteenth-century imperialism, Britain raced its rivals for colonial claims across the globe. The British extended their Indian empire eastward by conquering upper Burma in 1885, preempting a potential French advance from Indochina and opening the door to British merchants. Further east, British control over the Malay peninsula was enlarged in 1885 and 1888, again in anticipation of French intentions. Covetous eyes also turned to the archipelago of islands beyond Malaya. North Borneo became a British protectorate in 1881, with the same status extended in 1888 to neighbouring Brunei and Sarawak. In 1884 the British agreed to divide the island of New Guinea with the Germans, acquiring the eastern half (Papua), which skirted Australia's northern flank. The British also grabbed a clutch of Pacific islands, notably the Cook Islands in 1888.

A simple listing of the real estate that the British acquired obscures the sheer violence that conquest entailed. Indigenous resistance was widespread, generating the now all-but-forgotten 'little wars' that erupted along the continually shifting imperial frontier. Dozens of such wars broke out towards the end of the century. The establishment of colonial rule in Southern Rhodesia (Zimbabwe) offers a case in point. Three years after a heavily armed contingent of fortune hunters occupied the northern part of the territory, which was inhabited by the Shona peoples, colonial authorities engineered a war in 1893 against the independent Ndebele polity that ruled over the south, winning a quick victory. Several years later, however, the Ndebele and Shona surprised them with a coordinated uprising (1896–97) that killed a tenth of the white population and besieged the rest until reinforcements arrived and crushed the rebels. Here as elsewhere in the colonial realm arose an entirely new style of warfare, one that stood in marked contrast to the gentlemanly codes of conduct in Europe [*Doc. 1*]. The British possessed the technological means to wreak terrible havoc on their indigenous opponents: long-range rifles, machine guns, light field artillery, low-draught armoured gunboats, and so forth. When combined with a racialist dogma that dismissed Africans and other non-white peoples as hardly human, the stage was set for thoughts of genocide (Lindqvist, 1996). One settler in Southern Rhodesia voiced a common sentiment: 'I look upon the natives as merely superior baboons and the sooner they are exterminated the better' (Kennedy, 1987: 130). It also should be· noted, however, that the edge of urgency in this statement reflected the soldiers' and colonists' fears for their own survival. Anyone who has noted the innumerable memorials in British churches to loved ones killed in colonial wars will appreciate that the costs of conquest were not inconsiderable.

Once the British army or its various proxies (notably Indian forces) had crushed resistance, it became necessary to install a civil administration, which the British government initially preferred to subcontract if possible. It did so in several important instances by reviving what seemed a relic of the mercantilist era – the royal chartered company. This curious hybrid, a quasi-official commercial enterprise, was granted monopoly rights to the resources of a territory in return for shouldering its administration. The last of the old chartered companies had been swept away during the high tide of free trade – the British East India Company falling victim to the Indian rebellion of 1857–58 and the Canadian government buying out Hudson's Bay Company in 1870. But expediency brought the chartered company back into favour in the late nineteenth century, starting with the British Borneo Company in 1881. There were plenty of men willing to wager their fortunes on the rights to rule their own realm. The West African merchant George Goldie's Royal Niger Company tightened its stranglehold over trade in Southern Nigeria by acquiring a charter in 1886. On the other side of the continent, the Imperial British East Africa Company, financed by the shipping tycoon William MacKinnon, won the right in 1888 to oversee what would become Kenya and Uganda. A year later the British South Africa Company came into existence as a vehicle for the diamond and gold magnate Cecil Rhodes to establish dominion over much of central Africa, where his ego was writ large in the names of the new colonies, Southern and Northern Rhodesia [*Doc. 2*]. Chartered companies were rationalised as ways of injecting investment capital into newly acquired territories, but they appealed to the British government above all because they provided empire on the cheap. It was not lost on·liberal critics that the relinquishment of administrative responsibility to a private company opened the door to the unrestrained exploitation of native peoples, a problem that became especially apparent in the case of Rhodes's British South Africa Company. It was also obvious to the critics that these officially sanctioned monopolies represented a retreat from Britain's commitment to the principles of free trade. This was an early indicator of the corrosive effects of an increasingly competitive international climate.

THE IMPERIAL SYSTEM

With the imperial acquisitions of the late nineteenth century, Britain's position in the world became both more imposing and more fragile. The British Empire now comprised a vast array of territories that possessed widely varied political, economic and social connections to the metropolis. The so-called 'white settler colonies' of Canada, Australia, New Zealand and South Africa almost certainly held the highest place in the estimation of the average Briton, both because their institutions so closely resembled British ones and because their societies were so deeply dependent on British immigration. It is worth noting, however, that the 'white settler' designation was a rhetorical device that masked the presence of indigenous peoples, who ranged from an overwhelmed Aboriginal minority in Australia to an overwhelming Bantu majority in South Africa. The growing economic vigour and demographic size of these colonies garnered them greater attention from Britain's political intelligentsia in the late-Victorian era. Among the more influential works to trumpet their importance were Charles Dilke's *Greater Britain* (1868) and John Seeley's *The Expansion of England* (1883), which argued that the British possessed a special genius for planting their peoples, institutions and values around the globe. But this new appreciation came at the same time these colonies were acquiring increased control over their own political and economic destinies, giving rise to concerns that they would drift away from the mother country unless something was done to prevent it. The Imperial Federation League (1884) and other organisations were established to promote closer ties, and the first Imperial Conference (1887) of colonial and British leaders was seen by some as preparing the foundations for an imperial federation that could serve as a counterweight to the American and German federal systems.

Others regarded India as the keystone of the empire. It stood at the centre of an economic and strategic system that stretched from East Africa and the Middle East to China and Australia. Its markets absorbed a substantial – and growing – share of British exports and its own products helped to sustain the vital re-export trade on which British shipping built its international predominance. Its army enforced the imperial interests of Britain with interventions in Africa, China, and elsewhere. Its administration provided a template of autocratic governance that colonial officials from Malaya to Uganda turned to as they built their own structures of authority. India's importance, in turn, meant that the British were acutely sensitive to any threats to its security, and towards the end of the century such threats appeared to loom large with the expansion of Russia into Central Asia.

Although India would remain the 'crown jewel' of the dependent empire until it attained independence, it hardly required a visionary to see that the huge tracts of African territory that had been grabbed in the scramble possessed considerable potential. The problem was that the precise nature of this potential and the means needed to realise it were still not formulated. As for the rest of the formal empire, it consisted of varied bits and pieces – the languishing sugar islands of the Caribbean, the strategically vital naval bases at Gibraltar and Malta, the scattered coaling stations on islands dotting the world's oceans, and much more. Although their value to the empire varied widely, their composite significance consisted of a highly visible demonstration of Britain's global reach.

A series of late nineteenth-century technological developments made that reach much more immediately and directly felt than ever before. Stately sailing ships were driven into obsolescence by steam-powered vessels that kept to regular schedules and carried large cargoes in their strong steel hulls. Shipping times and costs plummeted while transoceanic traffic boomed, benefiting an industry dominated by the British merchant marine. The introduction of refrigerated holds in the 1880s opened to export an entirely new category of goods, allowing Australian mutton, New Zealand butter, South African fruit, and other perishable overseas commodities to enter the British market. The railway served a similar purpose on land, opening up new resources and markets to the international economy. The Indian rail system, started in 1854, was a remarkable feat of engineering that extended its reach to ever more distant corners of the subcontinent through the second half of the century. Canada completed its transcontinental railway in 1885, opening the prairies to commercial agriculture that flooded British markets with cheap grain. Railways served more explicitly imperial purposes as well: Kitchener's army built a railway up the Nile River as part of its methodical invasion of the Sudan, and control of East Africa was consolidated with the construction of a railway from the coastal port of Mombassa to the shores of Lake Victoria. Another technological advance that improved imperial ties was the telegraph, which was extended across the empire by means of transoceanic cables. The first line from Britain to India was laid in 1870, and the communication web culminated in 1902 in the Trans-Pacific cable, which established a direct link between Britain, Canada, Australia and New Zealand. What Daniel Headrick has termed the 'tentacles of progress' gave the British a tighter grip on their empire than ever before (Headrick, 1988).

These developments, of course, were not limited to the formal empire. British-built and British-owned vessels plied goods to and from foreign ports; British-financed and British-engineered railways snaked their way through independent countries. British economic and political influence ranged far beyond those areas of the map painted red. Through most of the nineteenth century, the unrivalled vigour of Britain's export-oriented industrial economy had been harnessed to its control of the seas and exercise of gunboat diplomacy to project its power and interests to regions of the world that retained their own – albeit often fragile – governments. Ronald Robinson and John Gallagher famously coined the term 'the imperialism of free trade' to describe this phenomenon (Robinson and Gallagher, 1953). Wherever possible, the British preferred to wield indirect influence on other countries through the competitive weight of its inexpensive manufactures, abundant capital and ubiquitous navy. Although the late nineteenth-century scramble for colonies had reduced the inventory of areas available to influence by such means, Britain still exercised considerable sway over much of Latin America, the Ottoman Empire, imperial China, and others.

In all of these regions, however, the British faced increased competition from rivals – from the United States in Latin America, from Russia and France in the Ottoman Empire, and from these powers and others in China. This competition was another manifestation of the intensified struggle for markets and spheres of influence that had helped to drive the scramble for colonies. And it signalled a significant restructuring in the global economy that carried troubling implications for Britain.

What was apparent to contemporaries was the way the terms of trade were turning against British producers. This was true above all for agriculture, which underwent a sustained depression from the mid-1870s as the technological triumph over the tyranny of distance allowed cheap foodstuffs from abroad to flood British markets. The consequent collapse in land values was a serious blow to almost everyone associated with the agrarian economy. The plight of agricultural labourers was worse than any other class of worker in late-Victorian society. The result was a widespread flight to the cities and in some cases to the colonies. Among landowners, those who suffered the most from the depression were the lesser gentry and other small-scale landlords whose existence was precariously dependent on rental income from tenant farmers: it was their sons who increasingly turned to the colonial services and the military as the prospects for a country gentleman's existence slipped away (Heussler, 1963). Land ceased to be the principal source of great wealth in Britain (Cain and Hopkins, I, 1993: 117).

Industry also flinched in the face of foreign competition, finding the empire a more congenial market for its goods as the Germans, Americans and others garnered increased market shares elsewhere (Alford, 1996).

Nearly 40 per cent of British exports were going to imperial ports by the end of the century, a noticeable increase on the proportion a few decades earlier. This trend was exacerbated by a series of international trade slumps in the late nineteenth century that caused most industrial countries to retreat behind protectionist walls. Germany introduced prohibitive tariffs in 1879, France in 1881, Italy in 1887, the United States in 1890. Some colonial governments, notably Canada and India's, followed suit. Such an economic climate made Britain's insistence on free trade principles seem foolhardy to a growing number of critics.

It has been commonplace for historians to trace the onset of British economic decline to this period. The industrial engine that drove the national economy is said to have slipped its track during the two decades running from the mid-1870s to the mid-1890s (Friedberg, 1988). Britain's share of the world market in manufactured commodities shrank from 25 per cent in 1880 to 21 per cent in 1900. And the national economy grew at a considerably slower rate than its rivals'. But it did grow: the British gross national product (GNP) increased from £1.317 billion in 1870 to £2.084 billion in 1900. The decline, in other words, was relative, not absolute. Moreover, it was mitigated by the continued vigour of British finance, shipping, insurance, and other 'invisibles', so called because they did not appear in the trade ledgers that provided the conventional measure of economic productivity. London entered its golden age as the financial capital of the world at the very moment that the Midlands were losing their claim to industrial supremacy. The massive amounts of money that circulated through the City gave it an imperial cosmopolitanism, attracting the English *rentiers* who lived off the dividends from Canadian railway and Malay plantation stocks, the South African randlords who built their fortunes on the speculative fever in diamonds and gold, and the various other aristocrats, plutocrats, parvenus, confidence men and common investors whose interests bound them to, or brought them from, distant corners of the globe. Recent studies have suggested that the financial sector was far more important to the late nineteenth-century British economy – and to its relationship with the empire – than the standard interpretation of the era acknowledges (Cain and Hopkins, I, 1993). If so, the claim that the increased emphasis given to empire was a response to, and a symptom of, the competitive weakness of industry is only partly right. The national economy underwent structural changes in the late nineteenth century that affected all sectors, not simply industry, and did so variably. Each of these sectors viewed the empire from a different vantage point, offering different assessments of its contribution to Britain. What was widely acknowledged, however, was that it did have an important contribution to make. Individuals in every sector of the economy had their own reasons for investment in the imperial system.

POPULAR IMPERIALISM

The empire became a more tangible presence in the lives of the British people towards the end of the century. This was made possible in part by technological advances in transportation and communication, but it was also a product of the increased importance of overseas possessions to the economic and political interests of various parties and the increased attention these possessions received from the press and other shapers of public opinion. The result was the rise of a new enthusiasm for empire that has been characterised as popular imperialism (MacKenzie, 1984, 1986).

Curiosity about strange lands and peoples was nothing new to the British: it was at least as old as the empire itself. What was new, however, was the ease with which that curiosity could be satisfied from the safety of British shores. People with imperial tales to tell were more plentiful than ever before. Missionaries on home leave detailed their struggles to convert the heathens of distant lands from the pulpits and in the periodicals of their churches and chapels. Explorers like Henry Morton Stanley became public celebrities, their lecture tours attracting huge audiences and their books becoming best-sellers – *In Darkest Africa* (1890) sold 150,000 copies almost immediately. A new breed of war correspondents provided dramatic first-hand accounts of colonial campaigns, dispatching them by telegraph for immediate publication in their newspapers. The military expedition sent to save Gordon had twenty reporters in its entourage. And the mass reproduction and dissemination of images in lantern slide presentations and illustrated newspapers brought the colonies and their inhabitants to life in ways that words never could. The impact of these varied influences on domestic audiences is difficult to measure, but impossible to ignore. This is especially true with regard to the countless invalided soldiers, retired officials, returned traders, and others who came back to Britain with curious trophies and strange tastes, each of them an intimate source of information about exotic lands for their families, friends and neighbours.

Nor was this growing familiarity with the empire entirely filtered through the experiences of Britons who had returned from overseas. The traffic between Britain and its empire was increasingly two-way: more and more colonial peoples were travelling to the imperial metropolis to work, to get an education, to lobby officials, to take a holiday, even to settle. London was the principal port of call, though most urban centres had some contact with colonial subjects. Visitors included supplicants from subject territories, such as the three Bechuana chiefs who came to England to lobby the Colonial Secretary to save their territory from the clutches of the British South Africa Company (Parsons, 1998). They included lascars (sailors) and other labourers from far-flung dominions who gathered together in semi-permanent communities in Cardiff, Bristol, Liverpool, and other port cities

(Tabili, 1994). They included large numbers of students from India and other colonies, among them the young Mohandas Gandhi, who studied law in London, and Cornelia Sorabji, the first Indian woman to attend Oxford (Burton, 1998; Lahiri, 2000). They included maharajas and businessmen, who gravitated to the centre of imperial power to promote their particular political or economic agendas. Common British citizens – cab drivers, boarding house keepers, and the like – came face to face with their colonial others. Reactions varied: some flung racial slurs at the dark-skinned strangers while others responded with curiosity and sympathy. The election of two Indians to Parliament in the 1890s – Dadhabai Naoroji in 1892 and Mancherjee Bhownaggree in 1895 – give one indication of the multi-ethnic dimensions of the imperial metropolis.

The empire was publicised and commercialised as never before for domestic consumption. Impresarios sponsored live shows at Earl's Court and other arenas around the country where the dramas of imperial conquest were recreated for the entertainment of audiences. The organisers of international trade fairs and exhibitions included model villages where Africans and other 'exotic' peoples were displayed in what were purported to be their native habitats. Museum curators prepared ethnographic exhibits of objects looted from conquered peoples, such as the Benin bronzes that went on display in the British Museum shortly after the 1897 war against the West African kingdom that created them. The music halls packed their stalls by performing plays and songs with imperial themes, stirring the boisterous, public expressions of patriotism that came to be known as 'jingoism'. The lyrics of one popular music hall ditty proclaimed:

> There are enemies around us who are jealous of our fame.
> We have made a mighty Empire and they'd like to do the same.
> And they think the way to do it is to catch us as we nap.
> While they push our friends and neighbours from their places on the map.
>
> [Chorus]
>
> And we mean to be the top dog still. Bow-wow.
> Yes, we mean to be the top dog still.
>
> (MacKenzie, 1984: 56)

The 'spectacle of empire' had become a pervasive part of late-Victorian culture (Coombes, 1994).

Various institutional and cultural forces helped to promote among the public a new appreciation of empire. One of the most important was the educational system. The elite boarding or public schools that catered to the sons of the middle and upper classes acquired an increasingly imperial orientation in the late nineteenth century, stressing service to the state, military training and national pride (Wilkinson, 1964). The extension of the franchise to working-class males in 1867 and 1884 created a political imperative to establish a system of schooling that would prepare working-class youths for their civic responsibilities. The curriculum designed for this purpose sought to replace class with national loyalty, and it associated the nation with a race patriotism that emphasised ethnic identity and empire (Heathorn, 2000).

Another important influence on public attitudes was popular literature, and towards the end of the century no literature was more popular than the imperial romances of Rudyard Kipling, H. Rider Haggard and Robert Louis Stevenson. Kipling, the hugely talented Anglo-Indian writer who burst on the domestic literary scene with his *Plain Tales from the Hills* (1888), was soon recognised as the bard of empire, especially with his poems 'Recessional' (1897) and 'The White Man's Burden' (1898), which gave memorable voice to the view that imperialism was a noble civilising endeavour that required a spirit of self-sacrifice from its agents. Recognising the importance of inculcating the imperial spirit in youth, Kipling turned some of his prodigious energies to juvenile literature. He entered a crowded field: G. A. Henty was the acknowledged master of the popular genre of 'boys' own stories', which had their girls' counterparts as well [*Doc. 3*]. These publications shaped young minds with their exciting tales of imperial derring-do and their racist representations of colonial peoples (Castle, 1996).

Channelling youthful energy and enthusiasm into activities beneficial to society was the purpose of the highly popular youth organisations that arose towards the end of the century, rallying their wards into quasi-military units that instilled discipline and a sense of duty. The prototype was the Boys' Brigade (1883), followed by the Church Lads' Brigade (1891) and various others, culminating with the Boy Scouts (1907), whose founder, Lord Robert Baden-Powell, drew directly on his own imperial experiences in shaping the group's ethos, activities and uniform (Rosenthal, 1986; Springhall, 1977). The attractions of these youth groups were just one of the ways imperialism and militarism influenced the late-Victorian corporate imagination. Christian evangelism took on an increasingly militant demeanour, especially so in the case of the Salvation Army, which made many converts with its uniforms, bands and marches, its agricultural 'colonies', and its assistance in migration within the empire. In the secular realm, several new academic disciplines honed their professional skills as intellectual adjuncts of empire. Anthropology, geography and tropical medicine sought to make the British better prepared to rule over their recently acquired colonies, and their efforts led to the creation of academic positions, professional schools, and other forms of institutional legitimation (Driver, 2001). The late nineteenth century also saw the establishment of a growing number of political and service organisations that promoted the empire as a source of material benefit and moral purpose. They included the Primrose League (1883), the Imperial Institute (1887), the British

Empire League (1894) the Imperial Federation Defence Committee (1894) and the Navy League (1894). The proliferation of these groups pointed to a sea-change in popular attitudes towards imperialism, which was measurable in the new and more positive connotations the term itself elicited (Koebner and Schmidt, 1964; MacKenzie, 1984).

One consequence of these developments is that the boundaries between imperialism and nationalism began to blur. The monarchy, the symbolic head of the nation, assumed a more explicit association with the empire. This was especially apparent at celebrations like Queen Victoria's Golden Jubilee (1887) and Diamond Jubilee (1897). These were 'imperial event[s]', elaborately staged ceremonials and parades that drew dignitaries and troops from every corner of the empire (Cannadine, 2001: 109). After 1887 Victoria's personal entourage included two splendidly costumed and turbaned Indian servants, and the aged queen took up Hindi lessons to give greater legitimacy to her claim to be Empress of India, a controversial title granted by Act of Parliament in 1876 (Burton, 1998: 51). Lord Salisbury's late-Victorian governments demonstrated that considerable electoral benefits could be gained from the association of nationalism with imperialism. Much of the success of 'Villa Toryism', the term used to describe the growing allegiance of suburban middle-class voters to the Conservatives, derived from the party's ability to tap into the patriotic loyalties of this class through its advocacy of an aggressive foreign policy. The Conservatives' inroads into this traditionally Liberal constituency were part of a general reconfiguration of politics in response to the rise of a mass electorate. The wild card in this deck was the new working-class voter, and although each party played a different hand in its bid for support, they shared a common strategic assumption – the working classes must develop deeper emotional and material bonds to the nation. With nationalism itself acquiring an increasingly imperial cast, this meant that the working classes had to be shown that they too could be the beneficiaries of empire.

FIN-DE-SIECLE ANXIETIES

By the final decade of the nineteenth century, imperialism's influence on the British domestic scene was readily apparent. Many of the social anxieties that afflicted the British arose out of a heightened appreciation of the precariousness of their place in the world, an appreciation that found its most visible expression in a new and insidious variant of social Darwinism. From the start, Charles Darwin's *Origin of Species* (1856) had inspired efforts to apply its theory of evolution through natural selection to the social and political realms. While the first generation of social Darwinists stressed the struggle among individuals within society, late-Victorian social theorists like Karl Pearson and Benjamin Kidd shifted the focus of analysis to the struggle between societies themselves, which they defined in national, racial, and other corporate terms. This emphasis struck a chord at a time when Britain's competition with rival powers for supremacy over the rest of the world seemed to be the prime determinant of world affairs (Semmel, 1968).

This 'external' variant of social Darwinism could be construed in several different ways. In its more 'optimistic' vein, it could be a source of re-assurance about Britain's international position and prospects. What better evidence that the Darwinian struggle worked in Britain's favour than its remarkable record of imperial expansion? And what surer confirmation that it worked against Africans, Asians, and others than their subjugation to colonial rule? Many of the so-called primitive peoples around the world were thought to be so poorly prepared for this struggle that they were referred to as 'dying races', soon to become as extinct as dinosaurs [*Doc. 4*]. Lord Salisbury held this view, insisting that 'one can roughly divide the nations of the world into the living and the dying' (Lindqvist, 1996: 140). He and his contemporaries were confident that the dividing line was a racial one, with the laws of nature operating inexorably against the darker-skinned peoples of the world.

Yet social Darwinism also supported a more pessimistic reading of Britain's fortunes. When the focus shifted from the struggle against dying races to the struggle against rising nations, the prospect that Britain would continue to stand at the top of the heap seemed far less certain. The growing economic and political influence of Germany, the United States, and other industrial nations was readily interpreted in terms of an inten-sifying Darwinian struggle for survival, which raised serious doubts about whether the British people were capable of victory in this struggle. The term that came to encapsulate these anxieties was degeneration: its shadow haunted the social vision of the late Victorians and Edwardians. It served as a central premise for some of the most memorably disturbing fiction of the era – Robert Louis Stevenson's *Strange Case of Dr. Jekyll and Mr. Hyde* (1886), Oscar Wilde's *Picture of Dorian Gray* (1891), and H. G. Well's *Time Machine* (1895). While Stevenson and Wilde inspired horror with their tales of the moral degeneration of a doctor and an artist, Wells touched the most sensitive nerve with his cautionary fantasy about a future in which the lower classes had degenerated into savage, subterranean beasts. Those who worried about the fate of the nation tended to focus their concern on the urban poor, a class of people bred in ignorance, violence and disease, deformed by adulterated foods and overcrowded housing. Social investi-gators like Charles Booth supplied first-hand evidence of the scale of the problem. A degenerate working class posed dire prospects for the struggle against rival states.

This social Darwinist perspective lent itself to a view of the urban poor as analogous to colonised peoples (Driver, 2001). Much of the social commentary of the time portrayed them in terms of physical difference, referring to their dark skins, low brows, and other marks of inferiority. The same impulses that sent Christian missionaries to Africa and Asia inspired the founding of missions in London's East End and other centres of urban squalor. The title that William Booth, the founder of the Salvation Army, chose for his best-selling book on the problem of poverty in late-Victorian Britain – *In Darkest England and the Way Out* (1890) – deliberately evoked images of 'darkest' Africa [*Doc. 5*]. His solution was equally infused by imperialism: the poor should be provided with assisted passages to the colonies. Most of the philanthropic societies of the late nineteenth century encouraged colonial emigration, especially by those young and resilient enough to overcome the degenerative effects of their degraded origins. Underlying these efforts was the conviction that the empire offered an escape valve for social pressures that otherwise threatened to spark class warfare. Cecil Rhodes put the matter bluntly: 'If you want to avoid civil war, you must become imperialists' (Semmel, 1968: 4).

Gender, like class, acquired an increasingly imperial inflection. The British had long pointed to the oppression of women in Africa, India, and elsewhere as evidence of the inferiority of these societies and their need for imperial oversight, but in the face of the late-Victorian feminist challenge to gender norms, this discourse served an increasingly domestic purpose as well, showing that women at home had it pretty good. Feminists, however, were adept at turning this discourse to their own ends, arguing that they too could make a contribution to the civilising mission on behalf of oppressed women overseas if they themselves were granted greater oppor-tunities to exercise their talents in the public sphere (Burton, 1994). They were also well aware of the ways in which imperial practices mirrored domestic ones in creating structures of patriarchy that oppressed women: Josephine Butler and her feminist supporters followed up their success in overturning the British Contagious Diseases Acts, which had targeted women as the carriers of disease, by turning their campaign against equi-valent venereal disease laws in India and other colonies (Levine, 1996).

The struggle over the role and status of women was also informed by rising concerns about the demographic disparity between the sexes in Britain, where the excess of women over men posed what was widely referred to as the 'spinster problem'. For the reproductive capacities of these women to go to waste for lack of men was seen as subversive both to their own moral purpose as mothers and to the social needs of the nation, which required an ever-expanding population if it hoped to keep pace with its rapidly growing rivals. One solution to this problem was to send 'surplus' women to the colonies, where many of those missing men had gone. Some of the same voluntary societies that sent the poor to colonial ports had similar programmes for single women, providing them with chaperons, employment assistance, free or reduced passages, supervised hostels, and other benefits to ease their transition to new lands and lives. If they married, as anticipated, these women were figured to be fulfilling their biologically appointed role, which brought the added bonus of bringing the refinements of domesticity to the lives of their husbands. Moreover, the colonies where they established residence would benefit from their productive and reproductive labours while Britain would relieve a troubling social problem in a way that strengthened the bonds of empire.

Those bonds were especially important to the settler colonies, which required large numbers of British women to make them work. Canada, Australia, New Zealand and South Africa all encouraged the immigration of women, recognising that their presence was crucial to the establishment of productive, self-sustaining settler communities. The biblical injunction to be fruitful and multiply was taken to heart: British women in New Zealand, for example, reproduced at one of the highest rates recorded in the nineteenth century.

A rather different set of gender dynamics operated in the dependent empire, where a small British elite ruled over large indigenous populations. This was very much a male domain, which was in fact one of its attractions for many British men. Although sizeable pockets of British women could be found in India by the end of the century, they tended to concentrate in the hill stations, which were physically removed from the rest of India; these women were in any case far outnumbered by men. Colonial Africa was even more masculine in character. The misogynist Cecil Rhodes specifically prohibited white women from entering Southern Rhodesia in the early years of colonisation, and much of the rest of Africa was considered too dangerous for the 'weaker sex'. This suited many men, who were drawn to the colonial frontier precisely because it offered them a refuge from the feminine presence – and the feminist challenge – in Britain (Rutherford, 1997). They constructed their own imperial version of a gendered sphere, one that attributed feminine or masculine characteristics to dependent subjects in accord with attributes the British themselves despised or admired. Thus, the Bengalis were cast as an 'effeminate race' because of their supposed indolence, querulousness and cowardliness, while the Gurkhas were favourably characterised as a 'manly race' for their fierceness in war and obedience to authority (Sinha, 1995). The same distinctions were drawn regarding the inhabitants of other colonial territories. They reflected the imperial values of the British themselves, and particularly their association of masculinity with military might. It is hardly surprising, of course, that those who had won an empire through conquest would privilege the warlike qualities that accounted for their success. But the meanings and ramifications attached to such notions of manliness have only begun to be unpacked and understood.

What is clear, however, is that militarism supplied a further point of connection between the domestic and the imperial realms. British culture acquired an increasingly militarist cast towards the end of the century. This is evident in the introduction of rifle clubs and cadet training programmes; in the popularity of the youth organisations and the activity of the Salvation Army; in the success of the adventure fiction of Haggard and Henty and others; in the jingoistic enthusiasms of the press and the music halls; in the public debates about foreign threats to naval supremacy and imperial security. The British soldier, previously a despised figure, became a national icon, ennobled by Kipling and others as 'Tommy', the simple, self-sacrificing guardian of the empire [*Doc.* 6]. This glorification of militarism was sustained by a social Darwinist vision that viewed international struggle as inevitable and war as an instrument of progress. With the boundaries between Britain and the larger world becoming ever more blurred, British society was increasingly informed by the sense that its survival compelled it to remake itself in preparation for the inevitable cataclysm.

One well-known historian writing about the period discussed in this book claims that the British 'were not an imperially minded people' (Beloff, 1970: 19). This statement sounds more like wishful thinking than an objective assessment of reality. Though there were, to be sure, some Britons who expressed moral or political revulsion to imperialism and others whose lives were too narrowly circumscribed to be conscious of its influence, the empire's presence in the domestic scene is too abundant to ignore. Whatever dimension of British life one wishes to consider – the political, the economic, the social, the cultural, the ideological – the markings of empire were there to be seen.

CHAPTER THREE

MAKING THE NATION IMPERIAL, 1900–14

For many Britons the new century brought more anxiety than hope. Though this anxiety derived from disparate sources – setbacks in a colonial war, competition in the international marketplace, challenges from global rivals, tensions in the social sphere – it found expression in forebodings of national decline, which was measured most often in terms of imperial power. Joseph Chamberlain gave portentous voice to this view when he proclaimed at the Imperial Conference of 1902: 'The Weary Titan staggers under the too vast orb of his fate' (Beloff, 1970: 83).

Many historians have characterised the era in terms that echo the concerns of Chamberlain and his contemporaries. They have portrayed Edwardian England as drifting inexorably towards disaster as industrial decline, social conflict and international entanglements culminated in the First World War. Their interpretations fix the blame on various targets – the loss of will among political and business elites, the failures of educational and economic institutions to modernise, the short-sighted commitments to imperial and defence structures (Barnett, 1972; Friedberg, 1988; Orde, 1996). Another argument turns these charges on their head by suggesting that delusions of grandeur prevented the British from recognising that their decline relative to rival powers was unavoidable (Holland, 1991).

Others have questioned the premises that underlie these pessimistic claims. P. J. Cain and A. G. Hopkins insist that industry was never as important to the British economy as most historians have assumed, and whatever weaknesses it exhibited in the Edwardian years were more than compensated for by the vigour of the financial and service sectors, whose international reach supported the continued advancement of British interests (Cain and Hopkins, I, 1993). Their analysis stresses the resilience of the British economy and the complexity of its alignments to social and political forces at home and abroad. It challenges the view that the trajectory of events can be traced downhill all the way. Much the same point has been made about the apparent deterioration of Britain's strategic position: many of the most serious threats to its security at the start of the century had been 'squared' by 1914 (Porter, 1996). This is not to say that other enemies did not take their place or that long-term trends were not worrying, but rather to observe that the outcome was not preordained. Britain's fortunes were flexible and contingent on an unpredictable array of factors. On one matter, however, nearly everyone agrees: Britain's fortunes were inextricably bound for better or for worse to its empire.

THE SOUTH AFRICAN WAR AND ITS AFTERMATH

No event was more responsible for raising doubts about the nation's future than the South African War (1899–1902). The simple fact that some 60,000 rough-hewn farmers of mainly Dutch extraction – Afrikaners, or Boers, who in the eyes of many Britons were scarcely superior to the indigenous peoples with whom they competed for southern Africa's resources – were able to withstand the full brunt of the crown's military might for nearly three years caused a great deal of consternation among the nation's political and intellectual leaders. The unexpected ordeal had widespread ramifications both at home and abroad.

The war was the culmination of long-standing tensions between the British and the Afrikaners of the Transvaal and, to a lesser extent, those of the Orange Free State. What caused those tensions to erupt into armed conflict have been the subject of debate from the start, and historians seem little closer to consensus on the matter than those who flung charges at one another in the midst of the war. One of the most influential analyses to appear at the time was the journalist and economist J. A. Hobson's contention that a cabal of capitalists had conspired to drag Britain into war to protect its investments in the Transvaal gold mines [*Doc. 7*]. Such suspicions were understandable in light of the fact that Cecil Rhodes, the best known of South Africa's mining magnates, had cooked up the disastrous Jameson Raid, which failed to overthrow the Transvaal's Afrikaner regime in December 1895. The British government, however, insisted that it went to war to defend strategic national interests. This claim has been backed up by an influential work that details the government's preoccupation with the threat that Transvaal's overtures to Germany and other actions appeared to pose to British control of the strategically vital sea lanes to India (Robinson and Gallagher, 1968). But other historians have insisted that economic interests predominated, pointing, for example, to Alfred Milner, the High Commissioner in South Africa, who in their interpretation pushed the Afrikaners to war because he concluded that control of the gold mines was vital to British interests (Marks and Trapido, 1978). The most recent analysis of the war's origins discounts the importance of either the sea lanes or the gold mines in British considerations, but comes down in the end on the side of those who stress its strategic concerns about regional supremacy

(Smith, 1996). Unfortunately, much of the debate about the origins of the war seems to feed on a false dichotomy, supposing political and economic interests to have been mutually exclusive. At the very least, it is clear that any threat the Transvaal posed to Britain's strategic position in the region derived from the increased influence the gold mines gave to this previously poverty-stricken and peripheral state.

While the British had suffered setbacks in other colonial campaigns, none compared in scale or significance to the South African struggle. The military had anticipated a brief war requiring 75,000 troops and costing £10 million; the prolonged ordeal actually engaged some 450,000 British and colonial troops and set back the British treasury to the tune of £230 million (Smith, 1996: 2). The war started with a series of stunning military reversals for the British during the infamous 'Black Week' at the end of 1899. Although they soon regained their footing and forced the Afrikaners on the defensive, victory was achieved only after the use of scorched earth tactics that destroyed 30,000 Afrikaner farms and forced enemy non-combatants into what were referred to as 'concentration camps', where some 25,000 of them, mostly women and children, died of the epidemic diseases that flourished in these closed, unsanitary quarters.

Sir Henry Campbell-Bannerman, the Liberal leader, denounced these 'methods of barbarism'. His own party, however, was divided over the war, much as it had been divided by the earlier imperial crisis over Irish Home Rule. The Liberal Imperialist wing supported the South African campaign, while Gladstonian and Radical elements were repulsed by what they regarded as unabashed aggression against an innocent people. Those who objected to the war were taunted as 'pro-Boer', with its none-too-subtle suggestion of treason. An 'orgy of patriotism', which found its most fervent expression in the public celebrations that greeted word of the relief of the Afrikaners' siege of the town of Mafeking, carried the Conservatives to triumph in the 'Khaki' election of 1900 (named in reference to the military uniform they wrapped around their campaign) (Price, 1972: 1). As the war dragged on, however, doubts about its merits increased, and critics began to make some headway with public opinion. Equally important, they crafted a critique of the war that supplied much of the theoretical infrastructure for the subsequent anti-imperial cause (Thornton, 1968).

Britain also found itself the object of opprobrium among its peers in the international community, which viewed the conflict as an effort by John Bull to bully his way to supremacy in South Africa. 'Splendid isolation', the phrase that summarised the entrenched British attitude towards European diplomatic entanglements, seemed less splendid and more precarious than before the war. Diplomats began to take a hard look at their country's foreign policy, and their assessment was influenced by the new geopolitical arguments about the sources of national power that came from the pens of

the American naval historian Alfred Thayer Mahan and the British geo-
grapher Halford Mackinder.

The outcome of this assessment was a diplomatic revolution as Britain
began to seek out allies and pare back commitments. Concluding that the
British strategic position in the Western Hemisphere was no longer tenable,
the government signed treaties with the United States in 1900 and 1901
that acknowledged the latter's predominance in the region and reduced its
own military presence there to skeletal levels (Orde, 1996). In East Asia, it
made a mutual defence pact with Japan in 1902, allowing it to withdraw
most of its fleet to home waters. These shifts in diplomatic alignments
culminated in 1904 and 1907 with stunning agreements between Britain
and its historical rivals, France and Russia. The Anglo-French entente of
1904 was, David Reynolds notes, 'essentially a colonial agreement' that
resolved disputes between the two powers in North Africa and other
overseas territories (Reynolds, 1991: 75). A similar resolution with Russia
in 1907 came about as each power acknowledged the other's sphere of
influence in Persia, Afghanistan, and other points of tension. The one
power with which Britain was unable to reach accommodation was
Germany, despite overtures by Chamberlain. While it is clear in retrospect
that these fateful decisions took Britain down the path to the First World
War, they were intended to stabilise the new imperial order that had arisen
out of the late nineteenth-century scramble – or, in effect, to certify the
division of the spoils [*Doc. 8*]. It had taken the South African War, with its
demonstration that conflict on a colonial frontier could dangerously disturb
the international system, to set off this diplomatic earthquake.

The repercussions of the conflict in South Africa were no less profound
at home. Various post-mortems sought to determine why the war had gone
wrong and what could be done about it. The failures of command and
coordination in the military seemed especially glaring and led to the
establishment in December 1902 of the Committee of Imperial Defence,
which assumed oversight of strategic planning for the empire. A major
reorganisation and reform of the army followed several years later under
the direction of the Liberal War Secretary, R. B. Haldane. Meanwhile, Lord
Roberts, the general who had rescued the South African campaign from its
stumbling start, concluded that the war effort had been hindered by the
country's volunteer military tradition. After his return to Britain he helped
to make the National Service League (1901) into a powerful pressure group
that claimed 270,000 members by 1914. It lobbied for the establishment of
compulsory military service, as well as rifle clubs, cadet training programmes, and other measures intended to mould an 'imperial race'
(Semmel, 1968). The Lads' Drill Association (1899), the National League
for Physical Education and Improvement (1905), and other groups urged
the introduction of military drill as part of the school curriculum (Penn,

1999). These and other initiatives pointed to the heightened preoccupation with military preparedness.

Worries about whether the British people would measure up to the demands of their imperial obligations were reinforced by the revelation that large numbers of volunteers for service in the South African War had been rejected as physically unfit, among them 8,000 of the 11,000 volunteers from Manchester. In 1904 Parliament established the Physical Deterioration Committee to investigate the sorry physical condition of the population and determine how it could be improved to meet the needs of the nation. Its report recommended that the state take action to reverse the degeneration of the masses. Other government commissions were convened to enquire into other matters of public health, such as 'feeblemindedness' and alcoholism. The Eugenics Education Society (1907) pressed the state to institute measures to prevent those identified as unfit from producing children. It also lobbied Parliament to pass the Mental Deficiency Act (1913), which required the institutionalisation of 'mental defectives', a loosely defined category that could be interpreted to include prostitutes, paupers and others (Jones, 1986). The nation's health was also considered to be at risk from the influx of poor immigrants from Southern and Eastern Europe, particularly Jews. The Royal Commission on Alien Immigration (1903) called for controls on the entry of undesirables, and a watered-down version of its recommendations became law with the Alien Act (1905), which granted new deportation powers to the state (Holmes, 1988). Growing concern about the large numbers of Indian students in Britain led to increased surveillance by government authorities and efforts to require them to carry identity certificates. It also fed into fears of miscegenation, which were fostered as well by a more visible Chinese presence. The India Office urged registry offices to warn British women against marrying men from polygamous societies (Lahiri, 2000).

Much of the debate about the nation's fate came to centre on the role and responsibilities of women. In a characteristic statement, the handbook for the Girl Guides, created as the counterpart to the Boy Scouts in 1909, declared: 'Decadence is threatening the nation, both moral and physical. ... Much of this decadence is due to the ignorance or supineness of mothers' (Colls and Dodd, 1986: 214). Campaigns to improve public health often focused on women as the arbiters of domestic hygiene. Working-class women in particular became the targets of campaigns by philanthropic agencies, medical officers, and others who sought to make them better caretakers of the nation's future by instructing them in pre- and post-natal care, regulating their use of midwives, giving them prizes for healthy babies, and otherwise intervening in unprecedented ways in their intimate lives (Davin, 1978).

Whatever failings were attributed to these women, they at least were carrying out their biological duty to the nation. More worrying to many contemporaries were those mainly middle-class 'new' women who shunned the private role of wife and mother, seeking instead better educational and employment opportunities and injecting themselves into the public realm with their demands for the vote. These developments were profoundly disturbing to many Edwardian men (and not a few women), who were convinced that the survival of the nation was dependent on the willingness of both sexes to assume their 'natural' gender roles. The 'new' women's failure to do so was widely regarded as a contributing factor in the falling national birth rate, a demographic trend that eugenicists and others identified as the most ominous indicator of imperial degeneration and decline. Many of the women who were the targets of these criticisms, however, drew quite different lessons from the war [*Doc. 9*]. Their participation in the 'pro-Boer' campaign injected a new militancy into the campaign for women's suffrage, finding expression in the violent tactics employed by Edwardian suffragists like Emmeline Pankhurst and her daughters (Mayhall, in Fletcher et al., 2000). What had begun, then, as a post-mortem of the military setbacks in South Africa wound up affecting almost every aspect of British society in one way or another.

THE SOCIAL IMPERIAL STATE

For a time it appeared the South African War would clear the way for a major realignment of British politics. Liberal Imperialists like Lord Rosebery, Herbert Asquith and R. B. Haldane shared much the same sympathy for a strong and activist state as did Conservative Unionists like Joseph Chamberlain and Arthur Balfour. Both groups advocated the aggressive pursuit of British imperial interests abroad and an equally aggressive effort to establish a regime of 'efficiency' at home. The combination has been characterised as 'social imperialism' (Semmel, 1968). It was inspired in part by the growing conviction that the state should serve as an active agent of social good, a view that the Oxford philosopher T. H. Green had done much to legitimise, and in part from the pervasive social Darwinist conviction that the global struggle for survival demanded a much fuller and more efficient mobilisation of the nation's resources than the limited liberal state allowed. A similar conviction could be found among members of the Fabian Society, a small but influential organisation that was socialist in name but statist in inclination; its leaders, Beatrice and Sidney Webb, brought representatives of the three groups together in the Coefficient Club (1902) to forge a common agenda. The club was short-lived, however, and a Liberal Imperialist/Conservative Unionist coalition failed to materialise. (Scally, 1975; Searle, 1971).

The most important reason for this failure was Chamberlain's politically destabilising decision to launch his tariff reform campaign in 1903. Disturbed by what he saw as signs that Britain's standing on the world stage was slipping, Chamberlain seized on tariff reform as a radically simple remedy for the nation's ills, which he attributed to industrial decline, imperial disunity and social disorder. He proposed protective duties to prevent foreign imports from undermining home industries, imperial preference to keep the dominions from drifting out of the nation's orbit, and social programmes – funded with the revenues from tariffs – to dampen down class tensions and nurture a strong imperial 'race'. His proposals represented a daring break from the half-century-long political consensus in favour of free trade [*Doc. 10*]. It inspired a host of fervent supporters, who made the Tariff Reform League (1903) one of the most powerful extra-Parliamentary political organisations of its day, with over 600 local branches by 1910 (Thompson, 2000). But the tariff reform campaign also divided his colleagues, even driving the up-and-coming Winston Churchill into the Liberal Party. It also ensured that the Liberal Imperialists remained Liberal. Reunited and reinvigorated by their opposition to protectionism, the Liberals made a compelling case to the electorate that Chamberlain's proposals would simply drive up the cost of living, creating 'dearer bread'. Their arguments won them a landslide victory in the election of 1906. Once again Chamberlain had served as the precipitating agent of a political upheaval, and once again his motivations had been imperial. This time, however, he wrought on the Conservative Unionists what he had wrought on the Liberals twenty years earlier.

Some historians have seen the 1906 election as a repudiation of imperialism (Beloff, 1970), but it was more accurately a repudiation of the radical restructuring of imperial policy advocated by Chamberlain. The Liberals reassured the electorate that the free trade doctrines that had brought Britain its global dominance would not be abandoned. This seemed a head-in-the-sand attitude to Chamberlain and his supporters, but it was not unresponsive to the troubling shifts that had occurred on the world scene; it simply saw protectionism as more harmful than helpful to those sectors of the economy that bolstered the country's international position, particularly finance, shipping, and other 'invisibles'. The new government pursued the imperial interests of Britain with no less determination than its predecessor. Key Cabinet positions went to Liberal Imperialists – the Treasury Office to Asquith, the War Office to Haldane, the Foreign Office to Sir Edward Grey – and their initiatives were driven by much the same desire for social 'efficiency' at home and imperial influence abroad as inspired their political rivals.

The main difference between the two parties was the means by which they sought what, in the final analysis, were very similar ends. This was certainly true with respect to colonial policies. The Liberal government was just as eager as its Conservative predecessor, for example, to see the South African states unified under British suzerainty. But it repudiated the post-war reconstruction strategy of Lord Milner, which had sought to smother Afrikaner recalcitrance under the accumulated forces of British immigration, acculturation and administration. Instead, the Liberals reached an accommodation with their country's erstwhile enemies, restoring self-government to the Transvaal and Orange River Colony (the renamed Orange Free State) in 1907. Despite Conservatives' cries that the government had snatched defeat from the jaws of victory, its conciliatory approach turned Afrikaner nationalists like Jan Smuts into imperial loyalists and paved the way for South African unification in 1910 – the very goal the British had pursued since the late 1870s (Chanock, 1977).

Conciliation marked the Liberal approach to India as well. Under the imperious and polarising viceroyalty of Lord Curzon (1899–1905), the hitherto moderate Indian nationalist movement had grown more restive and violent, especially in reaction to Curzon's too-clever-by-half decision to partition Bengal along sectarian lines so as to give the less politicised Muslims a majority in the east. When the Liberals came to power they sought to repair the damage by granting Indians greater participation in government with the Morley–Minto reforms in 1909 and by reversing the partition of Bengal in 1911. Once again, their efforts eased tensions while advancing imperial aims.

Where colonial nationalism posed no challenge, Liberal policies were scarcely distinguishable from Conservative Unionist ones. In tropical Africa, for example, the common goal was the development of the area's untapped agricultural and mineral resources (Havinden and Meredith, 1993). Chamberlain set matters in motion by encouraging economic investment in these newly acquired 'tropical estates' and regularising the administrative structures needed to oversee them. The chartered companies that had served as agents of British power during the 'Scramble' were cleared away in East and West Africa, and loosely managed protectorates became closely governed colonies, creating a new demand for administrators imbued with a bureaucratic ethos of service to the state. The hitherto insignificant Colonial Service, which had supplied officials for the Caribbean territories and other colonial backwaters, acquired increased importance, offering a new avenue of respectable employment to upper-middle-class males from Britain (Heussler, 1963). Although it remained to be seen whether these colonies would prove economically beneficial to Britain, the initiatives set in place by Chamberlain were in most instances endorsed by the Liberal Colonial Secretary, Lord Elgin, and his dynamic young Under-Secretary, Winston Churchill.

It was the domestic dimensions of imperial policies that caused the most serious clashes between Liberals and Conservative Unionists. How was the government to pay for the expensive array of obligations assumed by the social imperial state? The Conservatives generally favoured taxes on consumption: this was at the heart of Chamberlain's campaign for protectionist tariffs, and the crucial reason it attracted so much support from a party that otherwise professed its allegiance to the doctrine of free trade. The alternative offered by the Liberals was to tax property, a proposition endorsed by a new generation of social theorists (Harris, 1994). What made this position particularly divisive were the rapidly growing demands that social imperialism placed on the budget. The Liberal government had to find new revenues to pay for social programmes like old age pensions, unemployment and health insurance. It also became engaged in an expensive naval arms race with Germany, which caused naval estimates to rise 50 per cent between 1907/8 and 1913/14 to meet the costs of construction of the new Dreadnought battleships. It sought to pay the bill through more progressive tax measures, which were intended to take a bigger bite out of those with propertied wealth. Asquith's 1907 budget was the first to distinguish between earned and unearned income, but the really fateful step was the decision by David Lloyd George, Asquith's successor at the Exchequer, to proposing death duties and a 'super-tax' on the wealthy in his budget bill of 1909 (Clarke, 1996; Semmel, 1968). The bill created a political firestorm. Conservatives were outraged by what they regarded as an assault on the individual's fundamental right to property. They lacked the votes to kill the measure in the Commons, however, so they did so in the House of Lords. This action broke a long-standing constitutional precedent that restrained the Lords from interfering with the budgetary will of Commons. It set in motion a political crisis that shook the very foundations of the social imperial state.

A campaign that Lloyd George characterised in class terms as a battle of 'the People vs the Peers' left both sides bruised and bloodied. The Liberals emerged from the two elections of 1910 with a severely reduced majority. Though they managed to pass the Parliament Act of 1911, a historic measure that eliminated the Lords' power to veto legislation, they required the support of the Irish Nationalist Party to do so. The price of that support was a Home Rule bill for Ireland. For the past fifteen years this volatile issue had simmered on a back burner. Conservative Unionist governments had sought to kill Irish nationalism with kindness, expressed more notably in the Wyndham Act (1903), which aided land purchases by tenant farmers. Their Liberal successor had been inclined to let sleeping dogs lie. This was no longer possible. Coming at a time when the political environment was already overheated, the introduction of home rule legislation set off a violent conflagration. The Protestant Ulsterite community quickly mobilised, making clear its determination to resist home rule by force if necessary. Conservative Unionists, already embittered by the

Liberals' legislative assault on property and emasculation of the Lords, abetted the Ulster resistance and argued that the government's actions revealed its determination to overturn the constitution and undermine the kingdom. The Liberal government, according to Andrew Bonar Law, the opposition leader, was a 'Revolutionary Committee' without political legitimacy (Mansergh, I, 1982: 223). For many Conservative Unionists, the democratic system itself seemed bankrupt; they longed for a 'strong man' to restore order, someone with the grandeur and authority of an imperial proconsul. Milner fitted the bill and flirted with the idea of leading the anti-democratic cause (Nimocks, 1968). When the Irish crisis came to a head in 1914, Conservative Unionists' respect for the rule of law had deteriorated to such a degree that they applauded when army officers stationed in southern Ireland carried out the so-called Curragh mutiny, refusing orders to move their troops north in anticipation of an insurrection in Ulster. Prime Minister Asquith described the situation as 'a complete grammar of Anarchy' (Dangerfield, 1976: 76; O'Day, 1998). The country seemed on the verge of civil war. 'Ireland', one historian has observed, 'was Britain's Algeria' (Louis, in Brown and Louis, 1999: 13). It had much the same effect on the British body politic as Algeria did on France in the 1950s, tearing it apart in ways that endangered the existence of the state itself.

EMPIRE AND NATIONAL IDENTITY

One of the foremost reasons Irish Home Rule provoked such consternation was because it posed unnerving questions about the nature of British national identity. Though Ireland's role in the United Kingdom had always been the source of some ambivalence, the main thrust of British policy since the Act of Union had been the incorporation of John Bull's Other Island. The fierce resistance to home rule by people like Chamberlain was driven by the conviction that Ireland was the crucial test case for drawing other peoples into an imperial-cum-national identity. If it failed in Ireland it could hardly hope to succeed in more distant dominions. Indeed, it raised the spectre of separatist feelings stirring in Scotland and Wales, a prospect that threatened to strike to the very heart of Britishness. Seldom had the stakes been so high regarding what it meant to be British.

The imperialists themselves were largely responsible for upping the ante on this issue. Their determination to broaden notions of nationality to incorporate the settlers of Canada, Australia and other colonies challenged the territorial conventions that conceived of Britain as an island nation off the coast of Europe (Thompson, 1997). What the Liberal Imperialist Charles Dilke had termed 'Greater Britain' summarised their vision (and showed that it was not limited to Conservative Unionists). They insisted that the metaphor of the nation as a family should include those overseas peoples who shared the motherland's language, literature, laws, institutions, and so forth. This interpretation of the nation bore more than a passing resemblance to the contemporaneous pan-German and pan-Slav nationalisms that were sweeping through Central and Eastern Europe with their claims that the bonds of ethnicity or 'blood' superseded the geographical limits of states. (If the emotional attachments that tied Canadians, Australians, New Zealanders and other colonials to their mother country could be institutionalised through political and economic mechanisms, a genuinely greater Britain might be forged, a transoceanic Britain better prepared to match the manpower and resources of those continental behemoths, Germany, Russia and the United States.)

This was not an unrealistic ambition. Overseas settlers showed considerable loyalty to their ancestral homeland, as the South African War had demonstrated: 10,000 Australians, 8,300 Canadians and 6,500 New Zealanders had volunteered to fight for the British cause. Distance was no necessary barrier to Britishness. New Zealand was as physically remote from the British Isles as any part of the empire, yet its settlers retained an exceptionally deep devotion to their mother country. There is little evidence that the sense of themselves as New Zealanders came at the expense of their emotional attachment to Britain. (Much the same can be said of their counterparts in other settler colonies; they 'saw no tension in being both nationalists and imperialists' (Eddy and Schreuder, 1988: 6). Just as it is possible to possess dual passports, so it was possible to possess dual identities.)

Migratory trends lent encouragement to those who wanted to strengthen the relationship between the settler colonies and Britain. Whereas the United States had been the preferred destination of British emigrants in the late nineteenth century, the Edwardian years saw a shift in preference to the empire, which attracted 55 per cent of all outgoing passengers by 1906, 68 per cent by 1910, and 82 per cent by 1912. Moreover, the rate of emigration picked up in the new century, as did the proportion of emigrants from English as opposed to Irish shores. Canada was far and away the biggest draw, but Australia and New Zealand got an increased influx as well. The Colonial Office's Emigrants' Information Office offered advice intended to channel emigrants to imperial destinations. A wide array of religious and philanthropic organisations provided free passages, employment assistance, temporary housing, and other services for those who wanted to emigrate but lacked the means to do so. The Girls' Friendly Society, the Salvation Army, the YMCA, Dr Barnardo's Homes, the Child Emigration Society and the British Women's Emigration League were among the fifty or so private agencies in Britain that shipped unmarried women, orphans, farm labourers and other poor and 'superfluous' people to the colonies, where they could be put to productive use. Women would find husbands, orphans families, labourers jobs, benefiting both themselves and the societies that absorbed them. Moreover, their migration would ease gender and class tensions at home and strengthen the cultural and economic bonds between Britain and its dependencies (Plant, 1951).

Assisted migration schemes were only one feature of a multi-dimensional effort to bring about closer union between Britain and its settler colonies. Chamberlain's campaign for tariff reform, with its call for imperial preference, was part of this endeavour. So too were his efforts at the Imperial Conference of 1902 to persuade the settler colonies to become more active partners in imperial defence; other avenues of association were explored in the following conferences of 1907 and 1911 (Mansergh, I, 1982). Most of the press provided a steady diet of propaganda on behalf of imperial unity. The mass-circulation *Daily Mail* marketed itself as 'the voice of Empire' (Thompson, 2000: 63), while in 1912 *The Times*, already well-known for its pro-imperial stance, came under the editorial leadership of one of Lord Milner's protégés, Geoffrey Dawson. A burgeoning array of social and political advocacy groups established their own particular niches in pursuit of the imperial cause. A group of aristocratic ladies founded the Victoria League (1901), which sought to organise women to promote closer relations between Britain and the settler colonies (Bush, 2000). The Compatriots Club (1904), founded by Chamberlain's acolyte, Leo Amery, was established to serve as the 'brain trust' for the tariff reform campaign, crafting proposals for an imperial *zollverein* or commercial union to forge imperial economic integration (Scally, 1975). The Round Table, founded in 1910 by another Milner apostle, Lionel Curtis, advocated political integration through the development of some sort of imperial parliament; it also published an influential journal of the same name, edited by Dawson of *The Times*. One of the most ubiquitous promoters of the imperial cause was Lord Meath, whose wide-ranging initiatives included the Empire Day movement, which used parades and other public events to raise popular awareness of the empire and its importance to Britain (MacKenzie, 1984). Enthusiasts like Meath, Curtis and Amery were fond of referring to the British Empire as an 'organic union', as though some sort of biological imperative drew its peoples together.

This was wishful thinking. The campaign for imperial unity faced formidable obstacles. Its assumption that Britain and its colonies existed in an economically complementary relationship, with the former producing manufactured goods in exchange for the latter's agricultural and mineral resources, was at odds with the increasingly industrial, urban trajectory of the settler colonies, especially Canada and Australia. And its assumption that these colonies' political ambitions could be channelled into some sort of metropolitan-centred political system was at odds with the increasingly assertive claims of colonial nationalists for political autonomy. Although the Canadians and their counterparts showed little desire for divorce from Britain, they sought a more open marriage than their partner envisaged.

Moreover, British efforts to forge an imperial nationalism that incorporated the settler colonies had a corrosive effect on relations with the non-white subjects in their dependent colonies. Though the empire had always operated in certain respects in a racially exclusionary manner, it became much more obviously and intrusively so as a result of the efforts to establish a closer union with the self-governing settler states (Metcalf, 1994: 219-24). The official decision in 1907 to adopt the term 'Dominion' in reference to these states was a telling commentary on the empire's widening racial gulf. We must not underestimate the degree to which these developments sharpened a sense of betrayal among westernised Indians and their counterparts in other colonies, collaborating elites who had embraced the empire as a liberal sponsor of modernisation and self-determination. Their sympathy for the British imperial project was difficult to sustain in light of the special relationship that was being forged with the settler colonies, framed as it was around an explicitly racialist understanding of national identity. As if to confirm this conception of imperial nationalism, the governments of Canada, Australia, New Zealand and South Africa all launched efforts almost simultaneously to establish whites-only immigration policies and to prevent non-white residents from gaining the political rights of citizens (Huttenback, 1976). What effects these actions had on those they were meant to exclude can be seen in the case of Mohandas Gandhi, who moved to South Africa in 1893 to start a legal practice. Although his initial loyalty to the British Empire was ingrained enough that he organised an ambulance corps in support of British forces in the South African War, his subsequent struggle against the racially discriminatory policies being erected by the South African government previewed the doctrines and strategies that would drive his powerful assault on British rule in India.

CONTENTION AND CONSENSUS OVER EMPIRE

The general thrust of Edwardian imperial policy from the South African War onwards provoked an increasingly vocal and coherent body of criticism within the imperial metropolis itself. Some of it came from colonial delegations that had come to London to seek redress for various wrongs. They pleaded their cases on the steps of Parliament and Whitehall, at the offices of newspaper editors, and in public lectures sponsored by civic and religious groups. W. E. B. Du Bois and thirty other black leaders came to London in 1900 for the Pan-African Congress, the first of its kind, organised by the Barbados-born lawyer Henry Sylvester Williams to protest against racial discrimination in the empire (Schneer, 1999). The hundreds of students from India and other colonies who were enrolled in Britain's universities and programmes in law, medicine and other professions acquired in the course of their studies a keener sense of their rights as colonial subjects – or, to put a finer point to the matter, a keener sense of how to articulate those rights in terms that resonated in British minds (Lahiri, 2000). This sojourn in Britain was critical in shaping the views of nationalists like Jawaharlal Nehru. The curriculum at Oxford required them to read Mill's *On Liberty*, Burke's *Thoughts on the Present Discontent*, and Milton's *Areopagitica*: 'It would have been hard to concoct a more explosive cocktail for the young intelligentsia of a country under foreign rule', observes a historian of Oxford and empire (Symonds, 1991: 261). Still, the fuse that set off the colonial nationalist explosion burned slowly. Most of the Western-educated colonials who found themselves in the heart of the Edwardian empire were polite about pointing out their hosts' failures to live up to their self-professed liberal convictions (Burton, 1998).

Some of the sharpest criticisms of colonial policies came from Britons themselves. The Christian humanitarian lobby identified with Exeter Hall pressured the Colonial Office to protect indigenous peoples against abuses by settlers, traders and others. Under the leadership of the Reverend John Harris, the Anti-Slavery and Aborigines Protection Society (a merger of two separate humanitarian bodies in 1910) was a vocal critic of the more egregious cases of forced labour and land expropriation in the colonies. The efforts of the Exeter Hall philanthropists were themselves condemned by the West African traveller and expert Mary Kingsley for perpetuating the smug sense of superiority that afflicted Western attitudes. She advanced a cultural critique of colonialism, stressing the need to understand African customs on their own terms (Schneer, 1999). Though she died prematurely of typhoid contracted while nursing Afrikaners incarcerated in a South African concentration camp, her life served as an inspiration to E. D. Morel, perhaps the most influential and successful guardian of African interests in the Edwardian era. Aided by eyewitness reports from British consul Roger Casement and shocking photographs of mutilated Africans supplied by missionaries, Morel organised an impressive international campaign against the brutal regime of King Leopold in the Belgian Congo. This in turn laid the foundations for a more broadly based critique of colonial exploitation by Morel. It also helped to convert Casement into an Irish revolutionary nationalist whose involvement in the 1916 Easter Rising would lead to his execution by British authorities (Hochschild, 1998). For the most part, however, these humanitarian initiatives were inspired by the desire to ameliorate the impact of imperialism, not extirpate it. Reformers like Morel believed that the economic development of tropical lands was inevitable and appropriate, and their main concern was to make it as advantageous as possible to colonised peoples (Porter, 1968; Rich, 1986).

Others crafted a critique of imperialism that was concerned with its adverse effects on Britons, not Africans or Asians. In *The Psychology of Jingoism, Imperialism: A Study*, and other works, J. A. Hobson argued that imperial adventurism was corrosive to Britain's political and economic institutions [*Doc. 11*]. By provoking jingoistic enthusiasms for military conquests abroad, it corrupted democratic politics, distracting the public from its common concerns and usurping the state on behalf of special interest groups, controlled by a sinister network of mainly Jewish financiers (reflecting a xenophobic, anti-Semitic streak that ran through much Edwardian thought). Moreover, it dangerously diverted into overseas investments surplus capital that could be put to better use to improve the wages of British workers, whose increased purchasing power would in turn, according to Hobson, stimulate economic growth. Although Lenin and other Marxists modified this analysis to argue that imperialism was the inevitable outcome and terminal stage of capitalism, Hobson himself maintained that capitalism could be reformed, making it more responsive to the needs of the working class. He held a similar view with respect to imperialism's effects on subject peoples. Hobson never advocated the wholesale abandonment of colonial possessions; rather, like Morel and others of similar persuasion, he preferred a more morally upright imperial policy, one that brought benefits to the colonised as well as the coloniser (Porter, 1968).

The distance, then, between those who identified themselves as critics of empire and those who saw themselves as its defenders often was not as great as either party imagined it to be. With a few exceptions, both shared the conviction that the British embodied a superior civilisation and that this obliged them to bestow its benefits on the peoples they governed. While the critics complained that those who set imperial policies and those who acted as their colonial agents too often lost sight of these obligations, this did little to shake their sense of commitment to the ideal of a civilising mission. What the imperialist Rudyard Kipling referred to as 'the white man's burden' was in the end virtually indistinguishable from the doctrine of 'trusteeship' that Morel and his compatriots favoured.

It would indeed have been a rare individual to escape the ethnocentric assumptions that underwrote the Edwardians' understanding of the non-Western world, and the fact that critics of colonial policies operated within this frame of reference should not cause their accomplishments to be dismissed out of hand. It should instead serve as a reminder that almost all elements of the British political spectrum remained enmeshed in the imperial web in the early twentieth century. It may have been possible to argue against the expansion or the abuse of imperial power, but it was beyond the reach of the imagination of contemporary Britons to argue against the continuance of empire itself.

The new century had begun with a traumatic colonial war that caused

CHAPTER FOUR

WORLD WAR AND SOCIAL IMPERIALISM, 1914–22

What made the First World War truly a world war rather than merely a European civil war was the fact that nearly all of the major protagonists possessed overseas colonies, thereby ensuring that their quarrel assumed global proportions. Even though the war's origins are traceable to the tensions among European states and its outcome was determined by the struggle on the European continent, its effects on Africa, Asia, the Middle East and elsewhere were profound. Vladimir Lenin was not far off the mark when he argued in his influential essay, *Imperialism, the Highest Stage of Capitalism* (1917), that the European belligerents were fighting over the redistribution of the colonial world.

As the state with the largest and most valuable empire, Britain had the most to lose from any such redistribution. And there is little question that the war in many respects did weaken its position as an imperial power, draining it of human lives and material resources, destabilising the markets that were its economic lifeblood, and drawing it into the self-destructive rivalries among European states that cleared the way after 1945 for the bipolar predominance of the United States and the Soviet Union. But far from reducing Britain's global reach, the war actually enhanced it, placing an additional million square miles and 13 million inhabitants in its grip. With the restoration of some semblance of international order by 1922, the British Empire was larger than ever before, assuming an unprecedented place in British politics and public life.

THE ASSETS AND DEBITS OF EMPIRE

When the British Cabinet declared war against Germany in August 1914, it did so in the name of the empire, committing millions of Africans, Asians, Australians, Canadians, and others to a conflict that appeared to have no direct bearing on their lives. Yet this presumptuous action did surprisingly little to stir unrest among the peoples of the dependent empire. Westernised elites were generally quick to make public expressions of loyalty, while peasants and others went about their daily lives without at first discerning much change. India confirmed its reputation as 'a British barracks in an Oriental sea' (a phrase attributed to Lord Salisbury) by mobilising the largest colonial army in the world. The manner in which the settler colonies, now referred to as Dominions, responded to the outbreak of the war gave advocates of imperial unity particular cause for satisfaction. Australia and New Zealand voiced immediate and enthusiastic support, offering far more troops than the British high command initially knew what to do with. The Canadians were not far behind in endorsing the British cause. In South Africa, a rebellion by Afrikaner irreconcilables was crushed by the Afrikaner-led government of Louis Botha and Jan Smuts, ending any doubts about that Dominion's commitment to the British cause. The war also diverted Ireland from the Home Rule crisis that had brought it to the verge of civil war. Ulster Protestants' divisive assertions of loyalty to Britain found a more patriotic outlet, and even Irish Catholics volunteered in large numbers. For Britain, the irony of the First World War is that it opened up an avenue of escape from its pre-war crisis.

The Germans understandably hoped that they could divert British forces from the European front by exploiting discontent among their colonial subjects, but efforts to do so largely fell flat. With the crushing of the Afrikaner revolt, the window of opportunity in South Africa closed almost as soon as it had opened. German agents were unable to stir serious unrest in Egypt or Persia, even after the Ottomans entered the war as their allies. Though the Turkish sultan also held the title of caliph, the spiritual leader of Sunni Muslims, his call to the faithful in the Middle East and India to rise up against the British went largely unheeded (though it did appear to influence an Indian regiment's mutiny in Singapore in 1915). The Germans tried to ship contraband arms to India to assist in the revolutionary Ghadar Party's intended uprising, but the British broke up the conspiracy. Scarcely more successful were German efforts to run guns to Irish nationalists. They played no substantive role in the Easter Rising of 1916, the only serious rebellion against British rule during the war. (In fact, the rebels' liaison in Berlin, Roger Casement, was deposited on the Irish coast by a German submarine in a last-minute bid to call off the uprising.) While the constituent elements of the British Empire could not be considered havens of contentment during the war, what discontent there was arose largely out of the enormous pressures of the conflict itself, not the fitful conspiracies of the Germans [*Doc. 12*].

Those pressures were most painfully felt in terms of the war's insatiable demand for manpower (Perry, 1988). The British, to be sure, shouldered the greatest share of the military burden, putting some 6,704,000 men (22 per cent of its adult male population) in uniform. The Dominions, however, made substantial contributions as well: Canada provided 458,000 troops

(13.5 per cent of its adult male population), Australia 332,000 (13.5 per cent), New Zealand 112,000 (19 per cent), and South Africa 76,000 (11 per cent), though the latter figure counted whites only; approximately 50,000 South African blacks served in labour brigades (Mansergh, I, 1982). (It is also worth noting in this context that the contribution by Southern Rhodesia's white settlers, though numerically insignificant, amounted to 40 per cent of adult male population!) As the war dragged on and its human costs mounted, the Dominions were transformed in significant ways. They were obliged to contemplate a turn from voluntarism to compulsion to squeeze out more recruits: New Zealand introduced conscription in 1916 and Canada did so in 1917 (provoking riots among the French Canadians of Quebec), but Australians voted against it in 1916 and again in 1917. The bloodletting shattered the feelings of deference that the Dominions had hitherto shown to the British high command: if these generals could send their sons to slaughter with such equanimity, then perhaps it would be best if such forces served in the future under their own officers, men who might be expected to have their interests at heart. Finally, the destruction wrought on Australian and New Zealander forces at Gallipoli in 1915 and on the Canadians at Vimy Ridge in 1917 had a searing effect on the psyches of the survivors and their country-men, leaving scars of sacrifice that contributed to the ideological construction of distinct national identities in these Dominions (Barclay, 1976).

India, the traditional hub of British imperial defence, also experienced enormous pressure to provide manpower for the war. Its army grew from 160,000 to 800,000 by the end of the war: the total number of Indians to serve in uniform during the conflict came close to one and a half million. Though it remained a volunteer army to the end, there is little doubt that the scale of the wartime mobilisation strained Indian society and streng-thened the Indian nationalist movement. The Indian National Congress and the Muslim League were drawn into common cause and British authorities were obliged to respond with promises of political concessions after the war. The other part of the dependent empire to endure significant man-power demands was East Africa, where the British fought a long and dispiriting campaign against the Germans. In a region where the absence of roads and the presence of the tsetse fly obliged the contending armies to move supplies on the backs of men, the campaign depended as much on labourers as it did on soldiers. No one knows exactly how many Africans were pressed into service by the British, though estimates exceed a million, and the death toll from disease and abuse may have run anywhere from 100,000 to a quarter million. The labour demands provoked a small but worrying rising in Nyasaland in 1915 and left a lingering bitterness against the colonial state across East Africa (Page, 1987) [*Doc. 13*].

The global scale of the conflict compelled the British to move troops and labour corps from one continent to another, creating an entirely new kind of imperial diaspora. Indian forces fought in Mesopotamia, Gallipoli, France, East Africa, Greece, and on other fronts. West African troops were sent to the Middle East. Wartime needs led to 'strenuous efforts ... to recruit labourers in all parts of the world for one or other of the theatres' (Perry, 1988: 35). Colonial governments sent African labour regiments to France and Egypt. Some 90,000 Chinese were recruited for menial work on the Western Front. Responding to domestic labour shortages, substantial numbers of West Indians and Africans came to Britain to work on the docks and in the munitions and chemical industries (Panayi, 1994). The sudden influx of so many non-whites into the country was unprecedented and its consequences were impossible to predict. Authorities worried that it might destabilise the racial order that secured the empire by giving black men sexual access to white women, not to mention a keener appreciation for the mortality of white men. Non-white troops and labour corps were rigorously policed to prevent miscegenation and mutiny (Levine, 1998). Though the particular focus of the officials' anxieties may have been misplaced, they had real reason for alarm: colonial peoples' exposure to the West under the pressure of war did produce shifts in the dynamics of imperial relations, undermining the power of racial hierarchies and inspiring new claims to citizenship (Tabili, 1994).

THE TRIUMPH OF SOCIAL IMPERIALISM

The war brought equally profound changes to the internal workings of the British state. A political system that had appeared on the brink of disintegration in August 1914 proved – perhaps not surprisingly – unequal to the demands of total war. As problems mounted in the production of munitions, the provision of raw materials, the distribution of essential commodities and, above all, the supply of manpower, politicians began to grope for new ways to meet the unparalleled challenges they faced. Their efforts led to the dramatic growth in the size of the bureaucracy and the duties it performed. They also led to several major reshufflings of the political deck, first with the creation of a coalition government in 1915 under the continued leadership of Asquith, then with the far more dramatic upheaval that produced David Lloyd George's coalition in 1916. The clear trajectory of these administrative and political shifts was towards a more rigorously social imperialist agenda (Scally, 1975).

An active, interventionist state was essential to the success of the war effort (Marwick, 1965). As Minister of Munitions in 1915, Lloyd George was one of the first to understand this imperative. He wielded power in a way that would have been unthinkable before the war, assuming control of munitions factories, regulating the distribution of strategic materials, and instituting a system of arbitration between labour and management that prefigured the corporatist model of the inter-war years. Though other ministers may have lacked the gusto that Lloyd George brought to this endeavour, they too found it necessary to expand the reach of the state. Authorities placed controls on wages, prices and profits; they rationed food and other vital resources; they took over the railways and oversaw the shipping industry. They were managing two-thirds of the nation's economy by 1918 (Cain and Hopkins, II, 1993: 49). The state also encroached upon its citizens' social lives in unprecedented ways. Its concerns about the reduced productivity of heavy-drinking workers resulted in legislation that hiked beer and spirit prices and restricted the hours pubs could stay open. Its apprehension that high infant mortality shrank the stock from which those lost in combat might be replenished led to the establishment of child welfare clinics, midwife training programmes, free milk provisions, and National Baby Week (MacKay and Thane, in Colls and Dodd, 1986). Its recognition that the recruiting stations were no longer meeting the man-power needs on the Western Front resulted in the introduction of conscription in 1916, thereby abandoning one of the most fiercely treasured traditions of British freedom, the volunteer army. For those who had long preached the gospel of national 'efficiency', such developments seemed to confirm the prescience of their views.

Social imperialism reached its zenith with the Lloyd George coalition. David Lloyd George is one of the most pivotal and controversial figures in modern British politics. A 'pro-Boer' whose withering criticisms of British aggression in South Africa first brought him to prominence, he became the architect of the most aggressively imperialist foreign policy that Britain would pursue in the twentieth century. A Liberal minister whose progressive budgets and populist rhetoric enraged Conservative Unionist grandees, he became the leader of a wartime government that drew its greatest strength from his erstwhile enemies. Paradoxes and political opportunism appear to roil his career. But its course seems less puzzling if we dispel ourselves of the misconception that his liberalism stood at odds with his imperialism. As we saw in the previous chapter, there were important points of convergence between the two doctrines. It was not entirely coincidental that the long-anticipated alliance between Liberal Imperialists and Conservative Unionists finally found its broker in Lloyd George, who had flirted with the idea as early as 1910. It took the crisis on the Western Front, however, to break the logjam and clear the way for a serious political realignment (Scally, 1975).

Lloyd George surrounded himself with ministers and advisors whose common denominator was their commitment to empire. Many of them had exercised authority in the colonies, which gave them a keen appreciation for the ability of the state to mobilise economic resources and engineer social change. The key members of the small War Cabinet that directed the war effort and determined war aims were the imperial proconsuls Lord Curzon and Lord Milner, supplemented later by the Afrikaner nationalist turned imperial statesman, Jan Smuts. Lloyd George's government also included the unregenerate unionists Edward Carson and Andrew Bonar Law and the Conservative imperialists Arthur Balfour and Austen Chamberlain (Joe's son and political heir). Alfred Harmsworth, the influential if megalomaniacal owner of *The Times* and *Daily Mail*, lurked in the wings: he too was an ardent imperialist. To provide counsel and draft policies, Lloyd George turned to a clutch of advisors who had honed their administrative skills in post-war South Africa as members and associates of Milner's 'kindergarten', notably Lionel Curtis, Philip Kerr, John Buchan and Leo Amery. As John Gallagher observed, 'it would be hard to find any more imperially-minded government in British history than Lloyd George's' (Gallagher, 1982: 86–7).

One of the government's goals was to strengthen the bonds between Britain and the Dominions. In this endeavour it was aided by the war. As the costs of the conflict drained Britain of its investments and dried up its markets, it became increasingly reliant on the empire to supply the agricultural and mineral resources it consumed and to purchase the manufactured goods it produced. In the years 1915–20, imports from Asia (mainly India), sub-Saharan Africa and Australia reached roughly double the value they had held in the period 1910–14, while those from Canada actually tripled. This growth in trade compensated for the decline of European, Latin American, and other markets – though a big exception was the United States, which saw the value of its exports to Britain triple (Porter, 1996). For imperialist ideologues, the trends of trade seemed to be tracking towards the imperial self-sufficiency they had long advocated. They were not content, however, to await the capricious workings of war. Availing themselves of newly acquired powers, they sought to strengthen the spirit and substance of imperial unity. They persuaded Parliament to give official recognition to Empire Day in 1916. They established the Empire Resources Development Committee (1916 as well) to encourage investment in and exploitation of imperial resources. They convened the Empire Settlement Committee in 1917 to draw up plans to provide ex-servicemen with free passages to the empire after the war. They steered the Imperial Conference of 1917 into endorsement of empire settlement by veterans and a trade policy based on imperial preference. They responded to Dominions' complaints about the lack of consultation in the war by creating the Imperial War Cabinet, which gave the Dominion premiers quasi-ministerial standing in the government. They envisioned this concession as the first step towards a closer constitutional relationship between Britain and the Dominions, a Commonwealth that might eventuate perhaps in an imperial parliament. They laid the groundwork for a range of important post-war initiatives regarding the empire.

WAR IMPERIALISM

[The Lloyd George government sought not only to strengthen the bonds of empire, but to expand its boundaries. It found abundant opportunities to do so.] Gallagher again put the matter pithily: ('The First World War provided a vast bargain basement for empire builders')(Gallagher, 1982: 87). Germany's colonies proved ripe for the plucking. Most of them – South-West Africa, Togo and Cameroon in West Africa, New Guinea and Samoa in the Pacific – fell to small, makeshift British and Dominion forces in the early stages of the war. Tanganyika in East Africa proved more problematic, but the eventual outcome there was never really in doubt. (The big prize, however, proved to be in the Middle East, and it is hardly coincidental that over 35 per cent of all the imperial forces that participated in the war were stationed here. While British interest in the region initially centred on the defence of the strategically vital Suez Canal and southern Persian oil fields, it soon grew more expansive, contemplating the partition of the Ottoman Empire itself (Adelson, 1995; Monroe, 1981).

For half a century or more the Ottoman Empire had been suffering what seemed to most Western observers a slow death, and when it entered the war they gave it little chance of survival. Britain quickly annexed Cyprus and declared Egypt a protectorate, putting an end to the pretence that it was still an Ottoman client state. Both Lloyd George and Winston Churchill came to believe that the best way to break the stalemate on the Western Front was to strike at the 'soft underbelly' of Europe, their self-deluded metaphor for Turkey and surrounding territories. When the various campaigns launched to that purpose in 1915 went wrong – disastrously so in the cases of Gallipoli and Mesopotamia – the British pulled back, content for a time to snipe from the desert edges of the Ottomans' domain. This did not prevent them, however, from preparing the territorial claims they would make when the war came to an end. The Sykes–Picot memorandum of April 1916 made it crassly clear that the British and the French intended to carve up the greater part of the Ottoman Empire for themselves. While resembling the late nineteenth-century agreements that partitioned Africa, what made this agreement different was its secrecy – at least until the Bolshevik revolutionaries who overthrew the Czar in late 1917 revealed it to the world. One reason the British wanted it secret was that they had made commitments to other parties concerning some of the same territory. As an incentive for Arabs to rise up against Ottoman rule, Sir Henry MacMahon, the High Commissioner of Egypt, had pledged in October 1915 that the British would support their desire for political independence. And in an effort to placate Jews who were thought to have influence on America's decision to enter the war and Russia's decision to withdraw from it, the Balfour Declaration of November 1917 had promised to implement the

Zionist dream of a Jewish homeland in Palestine. The British soon found they had tied themselves into knots with their various promises [*Doc. 14*].

How they proceeded to extricate themselves from this quandary was part of the larger process by which they worked to realise their wartime ambitions. Although the slaughter in Europe came to an end in November 1918, the dynamics that drove war imperialism did not diminish. Rather, they intensified as the defeat of the Germans and the Turks and the descent by the Russians into civil war opened up new opportunities for the British. The 1919 Paris Peace Conference established the precedents and procedures for determining who would get what from whom. Germany's colonies were distributed among the victors in such a way that Britain's gains were cloaked somewhat by the claims of proxies. South-West Africa went to South Africa, New Guinea to Australia, and Samoa to New Zealand. Both Togo and Cameroon were divided between the French and the British. Tanganyika, however, went exclusively to Britain, an acquisition particularly prized because it realised Cecil Rhodes's dream of a British African empire stretching uninterrupted from the Cape to Cairo. The conference also invented a new nomenclature that dressed these old-fashioned colonial claims in more modern guise as 'mandated territories', a pretence intended to deflect American criticisms of the scramble for war spoils. As the historian H. A. L. Fisher put it, 'the crudity of conquest was draped in the veil of morality' by the mandate system (Thornton, 1968: 197).

The same designs were directed towards the peoples who inhabited what had been the Ottoman Empire, but there the situation remained fluid much longer. Even though the Sykes–Picot agreement had endorsed French claims to Syria, the British made a pre-emptive effort in the aftermath of the war to install into power their ally Feisal, leader of the Arab revolt against the Turks. When this failed, Feisal was moved to neighbouring Meso-potamia (soon to revert to its earlier name, Iraq). For Feisal's brother, Abdullah, the British carved out a new territorial entity, Transjordan. This was meant to compensate the Arabs for the loss of Palestine, which was made a British protectorate where the wartime promise of a homeland for Jews was honoured, in part because British policy makers believed that Jewish settlers would provide ballast for British strategic interests in the region. As Leo Amery put it, the intent was to use 'the Jews as we have used the Scots, to carry the English ideal through the Middle East' (Louis, 1992: 22). A similar strategy informed British policy towards Turkey, the Anatolian remnant of the Ottoman state: the Greeks were encouraged by the British to take Thrace, a coastal city largely populated by ethnic Greeks, and push into the Anatolian interior. The intent of each of these initiatives was to install groups of people who could be counted on to operate as imperial clients in geo-politically important regions.

As Foreign Secretary, Curzon pressed to establish British control over the entire swath of territory that stood between India and Egypt. He took advantage of the Russian civil war to send patrols into the Caucasus, a flotilla into the Caspian, and probes into other parts of Russia's Central Asian frontier. He coerced the Persians into signing a treaty that gave Britain a dominant position in their country, ceding it control of their external affairs, finances and tax collection, communications and transport system and, most importantly, oil fields and refineries. The British tightened their grip on the small sheikhdoms that bordered the Persian Gulf and installed advisors to influence Ibn Saud, who had consolidated power in the Arabian peninsula. Taken together with the mandated territories carved out of the corpse of the Ottoman Empire, these initiatives aimed to give Britain an unassailable position in the region. They marked the high tide of war imperialism.

CRISIS AND RECOVERY

It was not long, however, before the post-war imperial ambitions of Britain collided with the political aspirations of the peoples it sought to control, both in the Middle East and elsewhere. Those aspirations had been building during the war and they were bolstered by the American president's pronouncements that national self-determination was one of the rights for which the war had been fought. A series of crises swept across the empire and its *faux* frontiers in 1919–21. In Persia, resentment over the unequal treaty the country had been forced to sign brought to power the anti-British Reza Khan. In Egypt, protests organised by the nationalist leader Saad Zaghul boiled over into riots and other violence. In Mesopotamia, a full-fledged rebellion broke out against British rule. In Palestine, the first serious clashes occurred between Jews and Arabs. In Turkey, the strategic use of the Greeks as surrogates for British power unravelled as Mustafa Kemal mobilised a resurgent nation. In Afghanistan, diplomatic relations with the British degenerated into the Third Afghan War. In India, violence flared in the Punjab and a mass-based campaign against British rule was launched under the imaginative leadership of Mohandas Gandhi. In Ireland, Sinn Fein initiated a fierce guerrilla war to drive the British out of the country. There was considerable cross-fertilisation among these movements. Kemal gave encouragement to resistance by Muslims in other lands; the Indian and Egyptian nationalist movements looked to one another for inspiration and strategies; Sinn Fein provided a model for Bengali revolutionaries.

Some historians have interpreted these concurrent events as marking a crucial turning point in British fortunes, driving them down the road to imperial retreat (Barnett, 1972; Beloff, 1970). Perhaps, but there is little to suggest that those who shaped British policy saw the matter in such a dire light. While obliged in the face of nationalist challenges to scale back the size of their post-war imperial ambitions, they conducted a strategic redeployment that aimed to secure the essential elements of their new-found gains while shoring up those pre-existing positions that had been eroded by the war. Thus, the manner in which the British managed these post-war disturbances was no less significant than the disturbances themselves. Their determination to maintain power led them to seek new formulas of coercion and conciliation.

Given the climate of violence created by the war, it is perhaps not surprising that the British were often quick to resort to force against those who challenged their authority. One of the most notorious examples was the Amritsar massacre (1919), which occurred when a British commander in the Punjab ordered his troops to fire on a peaceful nationalist rally, killing some 400 protestors and wounding more than 1,000 others. Another instance occurred in Ireland in 1920 when British forces shot twelve people attending a soccer match in retaliation for the murder of some of their number by Irish nationalists. Neither of these atrocities advanced British aims; instead they energised aggrieved opponents. But more often the iron fist had the desired effect, cowing those with whom it came in contact. The aeroplane proved a particularly successful instrument of intimidation in the post-war period: it could get to inaccessible areas quickly and cost the British fewer casualties and less money than the alternatives. Colonial officials brought in the Royal Air Force to strafe and bomb recalcitrant villagers in Mesopotamia, Egypt, Sudan, Somaliland, Afghanistan and India (Clayton, 1986; Jeffery, 1984). While this usually worked, its means were brutally indiscriminate, provoking some British observers to complain that their nation's conduct in Mesopotamia was no better than that of the Turks (Callaghan, 1997: 34). Where conditions allowed, the British preferred statutory coercion, which carried at least the pretence of legality, if not justice. India's Rowlatt Acts (1919), for example, gave officials wide powers to detain and imprison those they deemed troublemakers. Such methods, however, were not available to the British in places like Mesopotamia, where their authority was not yet institutionalised.

The British understood, however, that coercion alone was not enough. It had to be counterbalanced by a certain measure of conciliation, courting groups to act as allies. Following on promises made during the war, the Government of India Act was passed in 1919, creating a constitutional hybrid termed 'dyarchy' that gave Indians a degree of self-government at the provincial level. The main beneficiaries of this concession were the Western-educated middle classes, whose cooperation was critical to the working of the Raj. So too was the support of the princes, who retained at least some semblance of authority over their hereditary states: in 1921 a

Chamber of Princes was established as a forum for them to address all-Indian affairs.

The British turned to traditional elites to bolster their power in much of the Middle East as well. In Egypt they dampened the ardour of the nationalists in 1922 by replacing the protectorate with a constitutional monarchy, though defence and communications remained in imperial hands. Similarly, the installation of Feisal and Abdullah as kings of Mesopotamia and Transjordan respectively in 1921 gave the British presence there a mollifying Arab face. Where the real power resided was never in doubt. A smug Curzon observed to Milner:

> You and I agree that these Eastern peoples with whom we have to ride pillion have different seats from Europeans, and it does not seem to matter much whether we put them in the saddle in front of us or whether they cling on behind, and hold us round the waist. The great thing is that the firm seat in the saddle shall be ours (Darwin, 1986: 35).

Proof that the British held 'the firm seat' was provided whenever the elites entrusted with political power acted against imperial interests or lost control over their own people. In those instances, the British readily intervened. As Arthur Balfour explained: 'No State can be described as really independent which has habitually and normally followed foreign advice supported, if the worst comes to the worst, by troops, aeroplanes, and tanks' (Thornton, 1968: 191).

This formula did not work very well when the British were operating at the outermost limits of their post-war expansion. A Russian government revitalized by the Bolshevik victory in the civil war pushed Britain from its tenuous perch in the Caucasus. A Persian government revitalized by the leadership of Reza Khan tore up the coercive treaty the British had imposed on that country. And a Turkish government, revitalized by the rise of Mustafa Kemal, caused havoc for the British attempt to advance the irredentist claims of their Greek clients. Britain came to the brink of war with Turkey in 1922 when Kemal drove the Greeks from Anatolia. The Chanak Crisis, as it was known, climaxed with a humiliating climb-down by the British, who found little enthusiasm for their belligerent stance among the Dominions – and outright opposition from Canada and South Africa. Chanak remade Kemal as the father of modern Turkey (signified by his new sobriquet, Ataturk). Setbacks such as these, however, did not alter the overall outcome of the post-war crisis of empire for Britain. It coped with the instability the war had wrought and consolidated the most important of its gains in the Middle East, enhancing its dominance over the strategic and economic affairs of the region.

The imperial crisis that hit closest to home in this period was the one that *was* closest to home – Ireland. There the mounting pressures of the war had turned the tide of Irish nationalism towards those who favoured a full break from Britain. The Easter Rising of 1916 was their initial bid to bring this about, and though it failed miserably, the execution of the ringleaders made them martyrs in the eyes of many of their countrymen. The decision to impose conscription on the Irish in the desperate late stages of the war also played into the hands of the extremists. Their party, Sinn Fein, won most of the Irish seats in the post-war election of 1918, and it proceeded to establish an independent, parallel government that challenged the legitimacy of the one subordinate to Westminster. The struggle between the two sides soon degenerated into military hostilities marked by the virtual absence of rules or restraints. In their efforts to crush the rebellion, the British instituted martial law and formed the 'Black and Tans', an auxiliary force of war veterans that gained notoriety for its ruthless methods. (Their services were later put to use in Palestine and Mesopotamia.) With neither side making much headway in the war, negotiations started in 1921, with Lloyd George personally heading up the British delegation. The Sinn Fein representatives wanted an independent republic that encompassed the entire island, while Lloyd George insisted that Ireland remain within the empire and Northern Ireland within the United Kingdom. His position prevailed in the ensuing treaty: Ireland was partitioned, with the Protestant stronghold in the north remaining in the union while the Free State became a Dominion, self-governing but still symbolically subordinate to the Crown (Dangerfield, 1976). The contending parties' response to the treaty is telling. Though the outcome was met with ambivalence by both sides, the Irish slid into civil war between pro- and anti-treaty forces while most Britons closed ranks, concluding that they had made the best of a bad situation – as, indeed, they had. If Ireland had been the touchstone of imperial nationalism before the First World War, the Easter Rising and the post-war rebellion had persuaded even the most fervent unionists that their earlier ambitions on its behalf needed to be scaled back and reconfigured. The idea of an imperial nationalism was not abandoned, but the Irish settlement pointed it in a new direction, one less hierarchical and constrained within an institutional shell.

DECONSTRUCTING/RECONSTRUCTING BRITAIN

What influence these events had on domestic attitudes towards empire is difficult to determine. The emotional undertow of war patriotism must have carried some of the public through these post-war troubles, sustaining their faith in the British imperial cause, though others doubtless were determined to see the entire great power game brought to an end. Those afflicted with feelings of disgust and disillusionment, however, were responding in the main not to events in the empire, but to those in Europe, especially the horrific destruction that had been wrought on the Western Front. It is telling that the person who gained the greatest popular renown as a war hero in Britain was T. E. Lawrence, better known as Lawrence of Arabia. As a British intelligence agent who aided the Arab revolt against the Ottomans, his military exploits occurred in a campaign that was irrelevant to the ultimate outcome of the war, but this meant little to a nation that had hungered for individuals it could proclaim heroes. The romantic image of a lone Englishman, dressed in flowing robes, leading fierce Arab warriors on desert cavalry charges and railway demolition raids held an immense appeal for a public that had been fed on Boy's Own adventure tales of resourceful figures acting manfully in exotic imperial locations [*Doc. 15*].

A deeper level of association between Britain and its empire is indicated by the way the post-war patterns at home paralleled those abroad, generating much the same mixture of peril and promise. One of the overriding issues was whether the social imperial policies that had held such sway in the latter years of the war would be able to meet the very different demands that arose with the return to some semblance of peace.

The British domestic scene was soon wracked by social and political turmoil, much of it inextricably associated with imperial matters. The seemingly insatiable need for military forces to police newly acquired imperial frontiers and increasingly restive colonial peoples caused the government to delay the demobilisation of troops and pass an emergency conscription bill in 1919. When several mutinies broke out among soldiers eager to return home, authorities sped up the rate of release, but not before discontent in the barracks had acquired a radical edge. For several years thereafter, the Cabinet was treated to monthly reports on suspected Bolshevik-style subversion among ex-servicemen. It did not help matters that work was scarce for returning veterans. Unemployment reached record levels as the British economy slipped into a serious post-war depression. Discontent took a racial turn in Liverpool, London, and other port cities when riots broke out in 1919 against non-white residents blamed for taking jobs away from veterans: a 'reign of terror' was said to have existed in Cardiff (Holmes, 1988: 107–8). Relations between workers and employers unravelled and strikes proliferated, many of them violent and tinged with revolutionary rhetoric. The Labour Party adopted a new, more explicitly socialist constitution in 1918 that declared its goal to be the 'common ownership of the means of production'. Hitherto a junior partner of the Liberals, Labour quickly acquired mass support as British politics took on an increasingly polarized, class-based character.

Another reason for the improved fortunes of the Labour Party was the passage of the Reform Act of 1918, which extended the vote to all males over the age of 21 and most females over the age of 30. This legislative leap towards a modern democracy was taken to reward the contribution that those without the vote had made to the war effort. The logic that extended the suffrage to certain women bore an intriguing resemblance to the logic that promised it to certain colonial subjects: it granted the privilege to those women whose maturity and prior exercise of the local franchise (which the wives of householders had possessed for some time) indicated they would utilise it responsibly (Clarke, 1996: 97–8). For Indians who acquired the provincial franchise a year later under the Government of India Act, the question was what the British required of them to reach a similar level of political participation.

If the Reform Act can be considered a gesture of conciliation, other actions demonstrated the state's willingness to employ coercion against its citizens, though obviously not on the scale seen in the empire. A paramilitary Defence Force was established to meet domestic needs. Viewing labour unrest through the lens of the Bolshevik menace, authorities drew up plans to call on troops to prevent an anticipated general strike from degenerating into revolutionary disorder. Infantry and tanks were used against strikers in Glasgow and several striking miners in Wales were shot by troops (Jeffery, 1984: 24–5). The Alien Restriction Act of 1919, an extension of wartime legislation directed against Germans, was turned against the portside blacks whose presence had sparked race riots, allowing authorities to classify them as aliens so that they could be deported from British shores (Tabili, 1994).

The government also initiated a concerted campaign to get ex-servicemen, women, and others to immigrate to the colonies in order to reduce unemployment and its attendant strife at home while strengthening bonds to the Dominions (Fedorowich, 1995). In 1919 the Colonial Office created the Overseas Settlement Committee to promote empire migration [*Doc. 16*]. Under the inspired leadership of the imperial enthusiast Leo Amery, this committee instituted a flurry of free passage and settlement schemes in coordination with voluntary agencies and colonial governments. It spread the word about the opportunities available overseas to the press, among veteran organisations, and at employment exchanges. It provided financial assistance to ex-servicemen, domestic servants, agricultural workers, and others who sought to emigrate. It supported the various soldier settlement schemes that sprang up in Canada, Australia, New Zealand, South Africa, Southern Rhodesia and Kenya, offering free or subsidised farmland to veterans. While these initiatives met with mixed success, Parliament was encouraged enough by what it saw to pass the Empire Settlement Act of 1922, which committed £3 million per year to support empire migration. This act would prove to be one of the most striking legislative successes of social imperialism in the inter-war era (Williams, in Constantine, 1990).

In general, however, social imperialism did not thrive in the years immediately after the war. Though the government kept much of the infrastructure of the war economy intact until 1920, its ability to engineer the sorts of changes sought by the social imperial state was seriously compromised by the post-war depression and the heavy debt burden to the United States. The heady ambitions that inspired Lloyd George to promise a whole raft of domestic social reforms as counterparts to his imperial initiatives crashed on the rocks of economic retrenchment. The Geddes Axe, the infamous cost-cutting measures imposed in 1921 by a government committee chaired by Sir Alex Geddes, drastically curtailed the ability of the state to maintain existing social initiatives, much less undertake new ones.

Retrenchment also obliged Britain to reassess its international commitments. Even Winston Churchill, in his capacity as Colonial Secretary (1921–22), felt some remorse about requesting 'these appalling sums of money for new Provinces' (Adelson, 1995: 196). The deep cuts inflicted on the army by the Geddes Axe made its task of consolidating the territorial gains acquired in the war increasingly difficult. By turning to Indian troops to garrison its new imperial domains and indigenous elites to govern them, the British were to some extent making a virtue of necessity. The navy too was forced to pare back, and despite the government's efforts to get the Dominions to fill the void, the slippage was impossible to ignore. It was in fact enshrined in the arms control agreement reached at the Washington Naval Conference of 1921, when Britain abandoned its traditional 'two-power' standard of naval supremacy in favour of parity with the United States and an acknowledgement of Japanese dominance in East Asian waters.

By 1922 the conditions under which Lloyd George's social imperial coalition had operated over the previous six years were no longer sustainable. The budgetary evisceration of social programmes dismayed Liberals and Labour, and the imperial setbacks at Chanak and elsewhere angered Conservatives. A polarised politics of party reasserted itself, undermining the coalition and forcing Lloyd George from power. But the intervening years of war and reconstruction had profoundly altered the shape of British politics. The Liberals, diminished and divided by the rivalry between the Lloyd George and Asquith wings of the party, had lost their earlier standing as the leading progressive party. That mantle went to the Labour Party, though it had yet to demonstrate that it possessed the ability to govern. The main beneficiaries of the new political dispensation were the Conservatives, who regained the predominance they had enjoyed in the late nineteenth century. Though no longer identified with Unionism, which had been made moot by the partition of Ireland, they still saw themselves as the party of empire and, insofar as circumstances allowed, they pursued an agenda that sought to strengthen that empire as an engine of economic growth and as a source of ideological inspiration to the British public.

CHAPTER FIVE

CONCESSIONS AND CONSOLIDATION, 1923–37

The inter-war years are often dismissed as an era emptied of hope and darkened by fear. Scarred by one world war and shaken by apprehension of another, blighted by economic distress and burdened by its attendant social unrest, Britain is said to have shrunk into a shell, its timorous leaders seemingly incapable of meeting the challenges that confronted them. The bleak title of T. S. Eliot's famous poem, 'The Waste Land' (1922), perfectly captures the reputation that the era has acquired. It is, however, a misleading reputation. While the well-being of Britain was undeniably in doubt, especially in the 1930s with the onset of the global depression and the rise of the fascist dictators, it should not be supposed that the country was directionless and defeatist between the wars. It continued to play a leading role in world affairs and, indeed, through much of this period no serious competitors challenged its place on the world stage: it was 'the only truly world power of consequence' (Cain and Hopkins, II, 1993: 6). Though it found its range of options more limited than before the war, it pursued its interests with more energy and imagination than is commonly supposed. Above all, domestic and international circumstances dictated a position that played neatly into the hands of imperialists, who embraced the opportunity to place the empire at the very centre of Britain's strategy for survival.

AN EMPIRE FOR THE MASSES

Large crowds and loud acclaim greeted the opening in 1924 of the British Empire Exhibition in the London suburb of Wembley. Unlike pre-war imperial exhibitions, which were financed by private entrepreneurs for private profit, Wembley was subsidised by an Act of Parliament and intended to serve official aims, above all the promotion of empire trade, migration and association. Its scale was unprecedented: a dense network of colonial pavilions, 'native villages', and fun-fairs, as well as Wembley stadium itself, covered its 220-acre site. Some 17.5 million visitors entered its gates in 1924, followed by another 9.75 million in 1925. They attended concerts, parades, pageants, jamborees, and other public events that celebrated the imperial relationship. They wandered through replicas of the Nigerian walled city of Kano, a stereotypical Chinese street in Hong Kong, a 'traditional' village from Burma, and other exotic milieus that sought to bring the empire alive. They bought brochures and postcards and plates and other bric-a-brac – what marketing experts now call 'tie-ins' – that disseminated information about the exhibition and the empire it celebrated to a wider audience (August, 1985; MacKenzie, 1984).

The Wembley exhibition was arguably the most visible and ambitious attempt in the inter-war years to instil in the public a sense of pride in their empire and an appreciation for the benefits it bestowed [*Doc. 17*]. It was, however, only one manifestation of a much larger initiative to promote an imperial consciousness among the British people. Given the power that mass democracy invested in public opinion, those who sought to advance the aims of empire understood that they could not leave popular impressions of its importance to chance. And given the threat that labour unrest posed to social and political order, most dramatically with the 1926 General Strike, advocates of empire considered it imperative to the nation's survival to inculcate a sense of loyalty to the imperial state. They sought to influence public attitudes towards the empire through strategies that John MacKenzie has termed 'imperial propaganda' and Thomas August characterised as 'the selling of the empire'.

What better promoter of the imperial cause could its advocates hope to enlist than the king himself? Although the ceremonial association of monarchy with empire can be traced at least as far back as the Royal Titles Bill (1876), it attained a new level of engagement in the inter-war years. George V was highly conscious of his ceremonial obligations to the empire. Among the annual honours he bestowed on his subjects was a new category of recognition proposed by Lord Curzon in 1917 – the Order of the British Empire. He was the first British monarch to go to India, where he was crowned emperor at the Coronation Durbar of 1911. Although he never again ventured overseas, he regularly sent his sons out on imperial tours: Edward, the playboy Prince of Wales, was especially peripatetic, stirring much excitement – and not a few rumours of romance – wherever his royal party passed (Cannadine, 2001). In 1932 the king gave the first of what became an annual Christmas Day address that was broadcast live across the empire. The text, composed by Kipling, struck an intimate tone, evoking an image of the empire as a family, the king its father: 'I speak now from my home and from my heart to you all; to men and women so cut off by the snows, the desert, or the sea, that only voices out of the air can reach them' (Rose, 1984: 394). The Balfour Report (1926) placed the king at the symbolic centre of the relationship that bound the Dominions to Britain and the monarchy's importance to the Commonwealth was enshrined in constitutional law with the Statute of Westminster (1931). Fittingly, George V's dying words are reported to have been, 'How is the empire?'

If the monarchy supplied a hierarchical symbol of imperial integration, sports supplied an egalitarian one. One of the most enduring cultural consequences of British imperial expansion was the diffusion of British games such as cricket, soccer and rugby football, golf and tennis. By the inter-war period, organised athletic competitions involving individuals and teams from different parts of the empire had become increasingly common. Famous test matches that pitted English cricket teams against opponents from the West Indies, Australia and elsewhere were followed with great interest across the empire. Intra-imperial rugby matches drew large audiences as well. An imperial counterpart to the Olympics, the British Empire Games (later renamed the Commonwealth Games) held their first competition in Hamilton, Canada in 1930, the second in London (1934), and a third in Sydney, Australia (1938). These and other sporting events helped to educate the public about the empire and imbue them with an appreciation for its place in British life.

The imperial cause also enjoyed the services of a number of voluntary advocacy groups. Some organisations of Edwardian vintage, like the Victoria League and the Round Table, continued to thrive, but a number of new ones sprang up as well. The post-war economic slump gave renewed impetus to efforts to advance imperial trade. The Empire Development Parliamentary Committee (1920), the Empire Development Union (1922), the Empire Industries Association (1924), and the Empire Economic Union (1929) all came into being to strengthen the economic bonds between Britain and its overseas territories. The government itself got involved in this effort by appropriating £1 million per year to the Empire Marketing Board (1926), which took up the task of promoting the sale of imperial products (Constantine, in MacKenzie, 1986).

The diffusion of imperial ideas among schoolchildren engaged the energies of other empire organisations. The Royal Colonial Institute supplied empire-oriented syllabi to the Board of Education and sponsored a popular empire essay competition; the British Empire Union promoted the celebration of Empire Day and the teaching of imperial history in the schools; the Imperial Institute offered slide lectures to young audiences on a wide range of imperial themes; the League of the Empire sponsored an annual exchange of teachers between Britain and the Dominions to encourage closer ties. Maps that highlighted the British Empire by colouring its far-flung dominions in red became familiar fixtures on the walls of inter-war classrooms. Imperial propaganda was especially prevalent in the elite public schools, where the sons of the middle and upper classes imbibed an ethos of sportsmanship, service to the state and imperial pride (Mangan, 1986). The spy novelist John Le Carré, who was educated in this period at one of these schools (Sherborne), recalls: 'The expensive English schools that provided me with what we must call an education saw it as their duty to prepare us for the burdens of imperial rule. Once a term, a wandering preacher calling himself a career adviser would descend on our school ... and acquaint us en masse with the ways of colonial life in Malaya, Kenya and India' (Le Carré, 2000–1: 68–69).

Universities were drawn closer to the empire as well. Oxford, Cambridge and London had become the beneficiaries of special chairs and lectureships in imperial history and related disciplines, funded by the Rhodes and Beit Trusts, making these influential institutions key sites for the dissemination of imperial views. They also had become the centres of empire-wide educational networks, providing advisors, headmasters and lecturers for institutions from Australia to Newfoundland and putting a distinctive stamp on colonial curricula, especially through the influence of the Oxford and Cambridge Examination Boards (Symonds, 1991). Oxford and Cambridge had already been rich recruiting grounds for the Indian Civil Service for some time, and so they continued to be, but the inter-war years opened an important new avenue of employment for their graduates – the newer colonies in Africa and elsewhere that came under the administrative oversight of the Colonial Service and related bodies (Egypt and Sudan had their own administrative systems). These organisations specifically sought out the public school and Oxbridge-educated sons of shabby-genteel landed families to staff their colonies. By the late 1920s nearly all of the individuals selected for this new mandarin class came from Oxbridge (Heussler, 1963: 50). Oxford held particular pride of place: its association with the Colonial Service was reinforced by the year-long training course it introduced for cadets. 'Red-brick' universities like Birmingham and Manchester established a rather different but equally important association to the colonial services by training many of the specialists in agronomy, forestry, and other technical vocations that had come into greater demand in the colonies.

Most Britons had no direct connection to the empire, of course, but the influence of the media made it increasingly difficult for them to remain ignorant of its existence or its purported benefits to Britain. Newspapers, which remained the public's main source of information about the world, were controlled by a handful of men who were not hesitant to hawk imperial causes in their pages. Both of the leading press barons, Lord Rothermere (Harold Harmsworth) and Lord Beaverbrook (Max Aitken), were enthusiasts of empire, as was the Berry Brothers group, which owned the *Daily Telegraph*, the *Morning Post*, and other high-circulation dailies (August, 1985: 92–3). The commercial development of the radio in the inter-war years introduced an entirely new medium for the dissemination of imperial sentiments, though one that the government placed in the hands of a public monopoly, the BBC (British Broadcasting Corporation). It assumed an official stance of objectivity, but this did not prevent it from broadcasting programmes like readings of Kipling's poetry and performances of Edward Elgar's marches that presented the empire in a positive light, while ensuring that critical perspectives never got airtime. The first speech by a monarch to be broadcast on radio was George V's opening address to the British Empire Exhibition, which reportedly reached 10 million listeners (MacKenzie, in MacKenzie, 1986; Rose, 1984: 393).

Another new medium of communication that advanced the aims of imperial propagandists was the cinema. Because of its enormous popularity in the inter-war years, the cinema was seen as an especially effective vehicle for reaching and influencing the masses. The Empire Film Unit, established under the auspices of the Empire Marketing Board in 1930, produced hundreds of documentary films that sought to inform viewers about the empire and persuade them of its value to their lives. Far more popular, of course, were the many commercial movies – both British- and American-made – that told tales of imperial adventure and heroism. Among the titles that attracted audiences were *She* (1925), *The Four Feathers* (1929), *Sanders of the River* (1935), and *Lives of a Bengal Lancer* (1935). At the same time, the British Board of Film Censors ensured that the public did not see films that portrayed the British imperial experience in a negative light. It banned D. W. Griffiths' *America* (1924), for example, because it represented the American Revolution as the triumph of freedom (MacKenzie, 1984: 79).

The censors also suppressed any film that seemed to diminish the dignity of whites or blur the boundaries between the races, a policy that reflected an increasingly pervasive preoccupation with the maintenance of racial difference. The great bugaboo of the inter-war years was miscegenation. Officials worried that white women would succumb to the dark-skinned men who had taken up residence in British cities: Africans, Indians and Chinese were variously suspected of devious designs. In Cardiff, where a substantial number of lascars (non-white sailors) lived, the police kept tabs on inter-racial marriages and liaisons. In Liverpool, another port city, an association was established to address the issue of mixed-race children. What Paul Rich terms 'the "half-cast" pathology' generated demands for action by authorities (Rich, 1986). Groups like the British Social Hygiene Council called for racially selective eugenics measures. Even as unlikely a figure as Sir John Harris, head of the Anti-Slavery Society, warned that the dangers of disease and miscegenation required controls on black immigration. In 1925 the Special Restriction (Coloured Alien Seamen) Order gave the state the power to expel lascars from British shores. It was 'the first legislation directed solely against coloured migrants' (Bush, 1999: 207). While concern centred mainly on seamen and other lower-class non-whites, several incidents focused attention on high society. A stage production of *Othello* caused a public outcry because the black actor Paul Robeson kissed his white co-star, Peggy Ashcroft. The heiress Nancy Astor stirred equally strong feelings by openly associating with black men in Soho night clubs (Holmes, 1988: 155–7; Tabili, 1994).

Anxieties about miscegenation were fuelled by the spread of racist stereotypes. British popular culture purveyed derogatory images of Africans, Indians, and others. The 'yellow peril' was evoked in the character of Fu Manchu, the fiendish villain in Sax Rohmer's popular adventure novels (and the equally popular films made from them). Children's literature was replete with schizophrenic images of colonial peoples – loyal servants and needy subjects on the one hand, vile terrorists and brutal savages on the other (Castle, 1996). Racism shaped the attitudes of leading politicians: Winston Churchill often referred to blacks as 'niggers', Indians as 'babus', and Chinese as 'chinks'. None of these prejudices were new, of course, but there is reason to believe that they spread more widely among the British people in the inter-war years than ever before. This may have been due in part to the growing presence of non-white sailors, students, and others in their midst, but it was above all a consequence of their heightened aware- ness of empire itself. By bringing the empire more fully to the attention of the average citizen, imperial enthusiasts also brought increasingly into play the racialist assumptions and ideas that sustained the imperial order. If the masses at home were to be educated about the benefits of empire, it was necessary as well to teach them the obligations it required – the dangers it posed and which were posed against it [*Doc. 18*].

It is in the end impossible to determine with any accuracy how far the advocates of an imperial way of life were able to infiltrate and influence the consciousness of the British public. We can more easily enumerate the initi- atives that were undertaken than measure their effects. But the cumulative weight of the evidence supports the judgement of one historian of empire, who has stated that this was 'the period in which the British were most aware of their empire' (Lloyd, 1996: 284).

TRUSTEESHIP AND DEVELOPMENT

Though the case for empire had long consisted of a mixture of self- interested and solicitous claims, these were conjoined in a particularly potent manner in the inter-war years. Trusteeship and development were the terms of choice for those engaged in constructing what became the twin pillars of colonial policy. Sir Frederick Lugard's *The Dual Mandate in Tropical Africa* (1922) offered the fullest and most influential articulation of this agenda. Written after his retirement from a celebrated imperial career that ranged from India and Hong Kong to Uganda and Nigeria,

Lugard argued that Britain had an obligation both to develop the economic resources of its colonies and to protect their indigenous inhabitants from exploitation. By assuring readers that the British could do moral good and gain material rewards at the same time, Lugard sought to reconcile what were often considered incompatible ends. His own inflated reputation as a colonial administrator added to the argument's influence and his journalist wife Flora Shaw's formidable propagandist skills heightened its profile, ensuring that *The Dual Mandate* became 'the most influential book on colonial affairs in the whole inter-war period' (Hetherington, 1978: 4).

The self-interested side of Lugard's 'dual mandate' was not new: Chamberlain had made the case for the development of Britain's 'tropical estates' at the turn of the century. But it was only after the war that most African and some Asian colonies acquired the administrative and logistical infrastructures that allowed their economic potential to be tapped in a systematic manner. What had been tenuously held territories, ruled by rough-and-ready methods, were transformed into stable colonial states, staffed by professional civil servants imbued with an ethos of service and equipped with the apparatus of power. They built roads, bridges and ports to open up markets, introduced cash crops and new agricultural techniques to stimulate production, imposed punitive taxes and coercive regulations to generate labour, and offered up land and mineral rights as incentives to investment (Munro, 1984). Although colonial governments continued to operate for the most part within the customary constraints of fiscal self-sufficiency, Britain became increasingly willing to offer *ad hoc* loans and grants from its own treasury to encourage the economic development of its dependencies, budgeting, for example, £10 million in loans to East Africa and Palestine in 1926. Such measures culminated in the landmark Colonial Development Act of 1929, which established a regular fund that colonies could draw on to jump-start commercial production (Havinden and Meredith, 1993). With copper coming from Northern Rhodesia, tin from Nigeria, cocoa from the Gold Coast, coffee from Kenya, tobacco from Southern Rhodesia, rubber from Malaya, and so forth, Chamberlain's 'tropical estates' were finally beginning to fulfil their promise.

Trusteeship, the other half of Lugard's 'dual mandate', was no more novel in its essential character than development. It bore a distinct family resemblance to 'the white man's burden', sharing the same paternalistic belief in the civilising mission of the colonisers. Still, it struck a very different rhetorical chord than the older phrase, which carried the jingoistic echoes of pre-war imperialism. The legal connotations of trusteeship were better suited to the new internationalist stance the victorious powers sought to establish during the peace conference at Paris in 1919 and afterwards. Under the system of mandated territories they devised to cloak their war claims, the British and their allies portrayed themselves as 'trustees' to their colonial charges, assuming an obligation under the terms of their mandates to stamp out slavery, prohibit the importation of alcohol and arms, and otherwise better the lives of the indigenous inhabitants. These commitments were not all that different from the ones that had been made at the Berlin (1892) and Brussels (1895) conferences, where the partition of Africa had been certified, but they succeeded in swaying some of empire's most influential critics. Both E. D. Morel and J. A. Hobson gave their blessings to trusteeship, believing that it offered the best chance of protecting native interests, especially when carried out under the international auspices of the League of Nations (Bush, 1999). It says something, however, about the modesty of their expectations that they saw no reason to object to the appointment of Lugard himself as Britain's representative on the mandate commission, where he helped to shape its policies until 1936 (Hetherington, 1978: 47).

How did trusteeship actually operate on the ground? Since there was little difference in practice between the way the British ruled their mandated territories and the way they ruled their regular colonies, trusteeship had to be measured by other means. The colonial policy that came to be most closely associated with its objectives was 'indirect rule'. Here again Lugard's influence looms large: he had coined the term to refer to the system of governance he had introduced as High Commissioner of Northern Nigeria, where the Fulani emirs who ruled the region were allowed to retain the trappings of power so long as they accepted the advice of their new over-lords [*Doc. 19*]. Similar deals were worked out with the Buganda of Uganda, the Lozi of Northern Rhodesia (Zambia), the Tswana of Bechuanaland (Botswana), and other peoples whose traditional elites had managed to survive the trauma of conquest with their status largely intact. There was nothing all that original about these arrangements: they had been the basis of relations between the Raj and the princely states of India for more than a century, and the British resorted to similar strategies elsewhere, as circumstances in the Middle East demonstrated. But Lugard infused 'indirect rule' with an ideological fragrance that made it irresistible to several important constituencies. One was the mandarin class that carried it out. Professional pride encouraged colonial officials to imbue their actions with some higher purpose, and 'indirect rule' fitted the bill, framing their association with traditional ruling elites not in terms of their own administrative convenience but in terms of the preservation of their subjects' way of life. This was no mere rationalisation: many colonial officials came from landed backgrounds that set them profoundly at odds with their own industrial, meritocratic society and made them deeply devoted to the agrarian, hierarchical ones they oversaw (Cannadine, 2001). Curiously enough, the other group that found 'indirect rule' particularly appealing were British progressives. Ramsay MacDonald, leader of the

Labour Party, voiced a view shared by many of his colleagues: 'We ought to maintain what remains of the old order, taking in hand the rulers to protect them against well-known evils' (Gupta, 1975: 128). Their post-war disillusionment with Western civilisation and anthropological appreciation for other cultures helped to persuade those on the political left that the most humane way to handle colonial peoples was to interfere with them as little as possible, protecting their fragile customs and institutions from the uprooting effects of modernisation. This is what made opponents of imperial exploitation like Morel such unlikely allies of Lugardian imperialists (Howe, 1993) [*Doc. 20*].

There were, however, others on the left who complained that indirect rule simply shored up feudal elites, securing their archaic and autocratic regimes against all change. If the common folk were left in poverty, ignorance and oppression, whose interests were served by a policy that promised trusteeship? These critics had their own unlikely allies, large business enterprises like Unilever, whose economic ambitions ran into roadblocks from colonial officials fearful of their disintegrative effects on traditional societies. In Northern Nigeria, for example, most Western mining and other business interests were kept out. Shunned corporate suitors saw such practices as evidence that development had been forsaken by indirect rule.

At the other end of the administrative spectrum were those colonies occupied by substantial numbers of white settlers. The preservation of traditional societies was the least of their concerns, which subordinated any thoughts of trusteeship to the settlers' voracious demands on resources. The two main sub-Saharan examples were Kenya and Southern Rhodesia (Zimbabwe); a similar dynamic operated in the Middle East with Jewish immigration to Palestine. Kenya had far fewer white settlers than Southern Rhodesia, both in absolute numbers and in proportion to the black population, and although they fought mightily for political autonomy (even contemplating kidnapping the governor during one particularly contentious patch in the early 1920s), they never managed to extricate themselves from the oversight of the Colonial Office – or the scrutiny of humanitarian opinion in Britain. A 1923 White Paper even declared African interests to be 'paramount' in Kenya, though this did not prevent the settlers from whittling away at native rights. Rhodesia's settlers were much freer to subordinate the indigenous population to their purposes. The British government assumed less constitutional oversight of that colony's affairs, granting 'responsible government' to the settlers when the British South Africa Company's charter expired in 1923 (Kennedy, 1987). Underwriting this decision was the expectation in Whitehall that South Africa would eventually absorb its northern neighbour (Chanock, 1977). This looming leviathan was in fact the foremost example of how settlers' interests trumped the concern for trusteeship. Even though South Africa's blacks outnumbered whites five to one, political power had been entrusted upon unification into the hands of the settler minority, who proceeded to use it to alienate land and extort labour from the indigenous majority. By recognising South Africa as a Dominion, Britain was reaffirming the racial character of that designation.

India, however, had begun to challenge the criteria of admission to Dominion status. With self-government within the empire the professed goal of most Indian nationalists, the Dominions provided the main constitutional model for their efforts. This was especially so after Gandhi called off his first non-cooperation campaign in 1921. The mass agitation he had been able to mobilise died down as communal violence between Hindus and Muslims broke out, the alliance between the Indian Congress and Muslim groups collapsed, and the great leader himself withdrew from the fray for several years after being released from prison in 1924. Moderates within the nationalist movement regained the upper hand, running for election to the legislative councils opened up under the constitutional reforms known as dyarchy and demonstrating their skills as responsible parties in local and regional governance. They had to struggle, however, against the paternalistic assumptions that affected almost all sides of the British political spectrum. When the prominent feminist and social activist Eleanor Rathbone turned her attention to the plight of women in India in the late 1920s, for example, she defined the issue in terms that privileged the 'civilising' influence of imperial trusteeship, stirring strong objections from Indian feminists, who – unlike their British 'sisters' before 1928 – actually enjoyed the same franchise rights as men (Sinha, in Fletcher et al., 2000). And when the Simon Commission was established in 1927 to consider further constitutional reforms in India, the British government did not think it necessary to appoint a single Indian to that body. This action provoked such outrage among nationalists that the Viceroy, Lord Irwin, felt obliged to soothe Indian opinion by announcing in 1929 that the eventual outcome of responsible government would be entry into the Commonwealth on equal standing with the Dominions (Moore, 1974). Whatever mollifying effects this announcement may have had on Indians, it came as a shock to many British and Dominion leaders by cutting against the grain of a contemporaneous set of initiatives that had increasingly distinguished the Dominions from the rest of the empire as a racially select club.

CREATING THE COMMONWEALTH

By the early 1920s it had become clear that Britain could no longer presume upon the imperial loyalty of the Dominions, at least not as implicitly and arrogantly as it had done before the war. Canada and South Africa's blank refusal to back up the British during the Chanak crisis of 1922 was the most dramatic demonstration that things had changed, but there were plenty of other indicators: with the possible exception of loyalist New Zealand, all of the Dominions were growing increasingly assertive about their own interests. The Commonwealth system that the British crafted in the inter-war years to accommodate this altered state of affairs should be seen, according to its leading historian, as 'a response to weakness, not an expression of strength' (Holland, 1981: 1). Certainly it evidenced an acknowledgement that the old assumptions informing relations between Britain and its Dominions were no longer sustainable. But Joseph Chamberlain's apostles had been making this point for years, and when the crisis came they embraced it as an opportunity to formulate new and more lasting bonds.

The first task that faced the engineers of imperial unity was to remodel the constitutional infrastructure that established the lines of political interaction between Britain and its Dominions. Parliament still retained the theoretical right to legislate for the Dominions, and the laws passed by Dominion legislatures were still subject to assent by Britain's imperial agents, the governors-general (Mansergh, II, 1982). The Imperial Conferences and the Imperial War Cabinet had failed to evolve into the formal imperial federation that had been the hope of many advocates of empire, and the course of events after the war seemed to be thrusting the Dominions into their own independent trajectories. The mid-1920s marked the launch of an important initiative to keep them in the same imperial orbit. It began with the creation in 1925 of the Dominions Office, which represented an institutional affirmation by the British government that their affairs were separate and distinct from those of the dependent colonies, which continued to be handled by the Colonial Office [*Doc. 21*]. The following year saw the publication of the Balfour Report, a crucial document in the political evolution of the Commonwealth. Drawing on a formulation first proposed by the South African leader Jan Smuts in 1921, the report recommended that Britain and the Dominions be seen as 'autonomous communities within the British Empire, equal in status, in no way subordinate one to another in any aspect of their domestic or external affairs, though united by a common allegiance to the Crown, and freely associated as members of the British Commonwealth of Nations' (Mansergh, II, 1982: 27–9). This famous statement offered up 'a working ambiguity' that was designed to satisfy all the relevant parties (Holland, 1981: 66). To a remarkable extent it succeeded, supplying the language and the logic that stood at the heart of the Statute of Westminster (1931). This legislative landmark made what was already a practical reality – an association of autonomous states – a constitutional one as well, now formally christened the British Commonwealth of Nations.

These political developments were a triumph for Leo Amery, the inter-war years' leading spokesman for the brand of imperialism associated with Chamberlain and Milner. As Colonial Secretary from 1924 to 1929 he had pressed for the creation of the new Dominions Office and served concurrently as its first Secretary. He had been one of the most vigorous advocates of the view that an enduring imperial relationship between Britain and the Dominions had to be a partnership, built on bonds of mutual respect and mutual benefit. From his perspective, the Statute of Westminster was validation that imperial unity could exist in concord with political independence (Louis, 1992).

What gave activists like Amery the courage of their convictions was their enduring faith in the power of 'race' patriotism. They believed that the ethnic ties between members of the Commonwealth would trump the political particularisms of individual states when push came to shove [*Doc. 22*]. Hence, they regarded the Statute of Westminster's emphasis on common allegiance to the king as more than mere symbolism: it was the vital expression of this bond of blood. This racialist vision also informed their insistence on the importance of continued migration from Britain to the Dominions. The emigrant was regarded as the vital connective tissue of the Commonwealth. Hence the Empire Settlement Act of 1922, which committed £3 million per annum to assist empire migration. The other main purpose of the act was to provide a remedy for domestic unemployment, then hovering around 17 per cent. The Cabinet Unemployment Committee had endorsed 'overseas settlement as a means of relieving abnormal unemployment', and the full Cabinet concurred (Williams, in Constantine, 1990: 38). The Dominions, however, were not keen to accept impecunious immigrants, suspecting designs to 'dump paupers', and the numbers assisted were in any case too small to make a significant dent in domestic unemployment figures. But the Empire Settlement Act did help to shift the flow of migration in an increasingly imperial direction. Though fewer people left British shores in the 1920s than before the war, the proportion that selected empire destinations increased dramatically, comprising 70 per cent of all emigrants by the end of the decade. The contribution the act made to this choice of terminus is evident in the proportion of emigrants who received assisted passages, growing from 23 per cent in 1923 to 50 per cent in 1926–27 to 67 per cent in 1929 (Plant, 1951: 90–1). No state initiative was more illustrative of the imperialists' contention that the well-being of Britain itself was bound up with its empire.

However much faith policy makers placed in the Dominions' emotional deference to Britain, they never lost sight of the fact that the imperial relationship was rooted in differentials of power. Measured in purely military terms, these remained as weighted in Britain's favour as ever. None of the Dominions maintained defence forces of any significance. South

Africa probably had the largest military capacity, but it was dispersed in lightly armed units intended for internal security – that is, native rebellions. Canada's permanent army numbered fewer than 4,000 troops, Australia's fewer than 2,000, New Zealand's little more than 500. Their navies and air forces were no more than token entities (Barclay, 1976: 99). They still looked to London in varying degrees to safeguard their security. The imperial metropolis was hard-pressed to meet these expectations: its strategic commitments had become strained in the aftermath of the First World War, with the Geddes Axe (1922) drastically curtailing defence spending and the Washington Naval Treaty (1921) requiring the abandonment of the two-power standard that symbolised the Royal Navy's global supremacy. But at least through the 1920s the navy continued to provide a formidable shield for overseas territories, and Antipodean anxieties were further eased by the construction of the naval base at Singapore, advertised as the Gibraltar of the East. Moreover, the Indian Army supplied a manpower-rich, if armament-poor, bulwark of imperial security from the Middle East to the Far East (Clayton, 1986). Only Canada, standing in the shadows of its American neighbour, required little in the way of protection from Britain, which is one reason why Mackenzie King, Canada's prime minister through much of this period, often showed such independence. The other Dominions understood that their claims to political autonomy were ultimately underwritten by the imperial promise of protection.

The one realm of relations with the Dominions that remained a source of frustration for imperialists of Amery's stripe was economic integration. The Conservative government's decision in 1923 to campaign on a platform of imperial protection led to its defeat at the polls. When it returned to office after a brief interlude, the free trader and Liberal renegade Winston Churchill was appointed Chancellor of the Exchequer, restoring the gold standard and ending any hope for Chamberlain-styled tariff reform. The only government initiative the advocates of imperial economic integration were able to get off the ground was the Empire Marketing Board, which used various forms of advertisement to encourage British consumers to buy empire goods. The Labour government was even more committed to free trade than its Conservative rival. Only the onset of the world depression in the 1930s was able to break the grip of financial orthodoxy and open the door to the advocates of imperial protection.

ECONOMIC CRISIS AND THE POLITICS OF EMPIRE

The continuing sway of free trade doctrine over the two governing parties was illustrative of the broad-based consensus that shaped imperial policy through much of the 1920s and early 1930s. The Conservatives, who held office almost without interruption from 1922 to 1929, generally took a measured approach to empire, seeking to stabilise post-war gains, conciliate colonial parties and encourage imperial trade. The empire never figured prominently in the policy considerations of the Labour Party, which formed a brief minority government in 1924 and returned to office in 1929. It followed much the same path in imperial issues as its political rival, sharing similar convictions about making the colonies more productive and their subjects more 'civilised', though it showed greater sympathy for the struggles of colonial labour movements than the Conservatives (Gupta, 1975). With the collapse of the international economy, however, serious fissures began to appear in the political landscape with respect to the consensus on empire. What is most striking about these fissures is that they ran as deeply within as between the two major parties.

It was Labour's misfortune that the depression struck shortly after it came to office. Eager to assure the public that it could govern responsibly, the Cabinet reacted to the crisis in a cautious, fiscally conservative manner, insisting on financial rectitude even at the cost of high unemployment. These orthodox measures provoked a radical challenge from Oswald Mosley, a promising young member of the government, who argued in a 1930 memorandum for an array of initiatives to stimulate the economy, including the introduction of tariffs tied to imperial preference. When the Cabinet rejected his recommendations, he quit his post and shortly thereafter the party, taking some of Labour's talented young turks with him (Clarke, 1996). His dissatisfaction with the conventional response to the crisis soon would take him in a more extremist – and more imperially oriented – direction.

Dissension within the opposition Conservative Party was equally intense, and it was more explicitly oriented towards an imperial solution to the crisis. This 'new imperialist resistance' to the party leadership took two main forms (Williamson, 1992: 3). One was concern about concessions to colonial nationalists, especially in India. Conservative die-hards established the Indian Empire Society in 1930 to resist the movement towards increased self-government, which appeared to be picking up pace with the Viceroy's statement about dominion status and the Round Table Conferences on India's constitutional future. They viewed these developments as evidence of imperial decline. The other major preoccupation of the critics was that perennial favourite, imperial preference. The two great press barons, Lord Beaverbrook and Lord Rothermere, plumped for the cause in their newspapers, and Beaverbrook went so far as to launch an independent party, the United Empire Party, on an empire trade platform. Their solution to the economic crisis was imperial autarky.

Out of this unstable political environment arose the National Government in 1931. A coalition crafted by leaders of each of the major parties – Labour's Ramsay MacDonald, the Conservatives' Stanley Baldwin, the Liberals' John Simon – it represented a setback for critics of all stripes. Composed predominantly of Conservatives and cautious in character, the new government seemed set to continue the policies of the past. And so it did in its domestic agenda. But the pressures of the international economic crisis provided the impetus for the breakthrough that the proponents of imperial preference had been advocating for decades.

With the collapse of the international financial system and the retreat by many countries behind tariff walls, British and Dominion officials gathered at Ottawa in 1932 to devise a common trade policy. The outcome of the Ottawa Conference was that Britain abandoned its vaunted tradition of free trade and introduced in its place a system of imperial tariffs, placing preferential duties on goods imported from other parts of the empire; the Dominions reciprocated (Drummond, 1974). While trade figures show that Britain had become increasingly reliant on exchange with its empire for some time, the Ottawa agreement appears to have diverted even more trade into imperial channels. In the period 1925–29, the empire accounted for 28 per cent of British imports and 42 per cent of its exports; by 1935–39, the corresponding figures were 40 per cent and 49 per cent. It is generally agreed, however, that the Dominions got a better deal than Britain: they were able to export more goods to the imperial metropolis than it was able to export to them, widening its trade deficit (Alford, 1996: 144). This has led some historians to insist that Ottawa exposed the fallacy of imperial preference, which operated under the illusion that the British and Dominion economies were complementary (Holland, 1981). More recently, however, it has been suggested that the agreement's inequities were the price Britain willingly paid for a strong sterling area, the closed currency zone it instituted after abandoning the gold standard in 1931. With the collapse of any internationally recognised currency standard, the sterling area ensured that Britain retained its former financial leverage at least within the empire and among countries that pegged their currency to sterling, such as Denmark and Argentina (Cain and Hopkins, II, 1993: 87–93). Its value would become especially evident during the Second World War, when Britain was able to draw on the sterling reserves its trading partners held in London accounts to finance its war effort, and afterwards, when it provided a protected trade zone that impeded incursions by American commercial interests. In the midst of the depression, moreover, it is difficult to see what other viable alternatives were available to Britain.

Other imperial economic policies were instituted that interfered with the workings of free trade as well. In most African colonies, which depended on primary commodity exports, marketing boards appeared in the 1930s to act as buffers between local producers and an increasingly unfavourable international market. They originated in Kenya and Southern Rhodesia, where they were intended to prop up white farmers by purchasing their products at subsidised prices, but as they spread to colonies where indigenous farmers predominated their purpose changed: they became mechanisms to extract revenue from producers by paying them below-market prices for their goods. The result of this regulatory practice was that sizeable surpluses were accumulated by colonial governments and deposited in metropolitan accounts where they helped to sustain the pound (Munro, 1984: 36–7).

India too turned towards a more regulated economy, though the benefits the British accrued from this abandonment of free trade were more difficult to discern. The Indian government had enjoyed a good deal of fiscal autonomy since 1919, and at the onset of the depression it moved to protect home industries by imposing stiff tariffs on imports, including cotton goods from Britain, which produced howls of dismay from Lancashire. By the early 1930s the two parties had negotiated a system of imperial preference that paralleled the one worked out with the Dominions, and with similar consequences: the terms of trade turned increasingly in India's favour (Tomlinson, 1979). These growing surpluses, however, were accumulated in sterling, which circulated through London financial markets in the service of British financial interests. In this respect, too, the economic relationship between Britain and India bore a striking resemblance to the one between Britain and the Dominions.

Whether this resemblance would extend to the constitutional sphere was the most controversial imperial question to appear in the British political arena in the 1930s. After negotiating with various Indian constituencies at the Round Table Conferences (1930–32) and withstanding the effects of Gandhi's second civil disobedience campaign (also 1930–32), the National Government introduced a Government of India bill that proposed full self-government at the provincial level and an elected legislature with considerable powers at the federal level. Although it offered some real and substantive concessions to the Indian nationalist forces, the mechanics of its implementation and operation ensured that the interests of the Indian princes were safeguarded, making it in fact 'a highly conservative document' (Mansergh, II, 1982: 68). Gandhi rejected it out of hand. But so did some members of the Conservative Party, who reacted with alarm at what they regarded as a scheme to surrender the crown jewel of the empire. Led by Winston Churchill, they launched a fierce campaign to defeat the bill, causing Stanley Baldwin to conclude that Churchill had 'gone quite mad about India' (Charmley, 1993: 257). The bill's opponents were in the end unable to prevent its passage in 1935, but their efforts were threatening enough to kept Churchill out of office until the war started in 1939 [*Doc. 23*].

What gave the debate over the Government of India bill its heat was that it pitted against one another members of the same party who shared the same imperial convictions. Their disagreement hinged on how to maintain the empire. On the one side were imperialists like Leo Amery, who believed that the best way to keep India in the imperial orbit was to demonstrate good will by granting it self-government. On the other side were Churchill and his supporters, who believed that concessions to Indian nationalists were expressions of weakness that would lead to the dissolution of the empire. Churchill's stance has been seen by some as evidence of an erratic personality's retreat into reactionary politics, but his position had in fact changed very little from the past. If not a 'Mid-Victorian' in his views on empire, as Amery charged (Louis, 1992: 105), he remained very much an Edwardian Liberal Imperialist, faithful to the doctrine of free trade and acquiescent to white colonists' claims to representative government, but convinced that other races required British oversight. It was in fact the imperialists on the other side of the debate who were willing to chart a change of course. Recognising that the Indian nationalist movement could not be crushed, they sought a pragmatic solution that might satisfy its demands while maintaining their influence. This bold effort to reconfigure the imperial relationship was at the heart of the Government of India Act.

Apart from criticism of the India bill, the Nationalist Government faced little challenge from the right. Beaverbrook's United Empire Party lost its *raison d'être* with the Ottawa agreement. Oswald Mosley launched the British Union of Fascists in 1932, but support for its poisonous mixture of anti-Semitism, imperialism, militarism and totalitarianism rapidly shrank. The government's main critics came instead from the left, with the Labour Party's anti-coalitionists comprising the bulk of the opposition in Parliament. The empire, however, mattered little to most Labourites: except for occasional outcries against egregious cases of labour exploitation, imperial issues were left to the party's Fabians, who took a 'constructive' stance towards the subject (Gupta, 1975).

The only sustained attacks on imperialism in these years came from leftist fringe groups that had limited influence in the political arena. Both the Communist Party and the Independent Labour Party (which broke with the Labour Party in 1932) showed some interest in colonial resistance movements, and the latter group sketched out an economic critique of imperialism (Howe, 1993). Some of the colonial students and other non-white peoples who resided in Britain became increasingly politicised. A group of black intellectuals led by C. L. R. James and George Padmore from the Caribbean and Jomo Kenyatta from Kenya began to formulate a pan-African perspective that was actively anti-imperialist in orientation (Holmes, 1988). The Italian invasion of Ethiopia in 1935 gave a powerful impetus to these efforts, radicalising blacks across Africa and the Caribbean, where the Rastafarian movement (1933–34) regarded the Ethiopian emperor Haile Selassie as divine. But their concerns scarcely rippled the surface in Britain itself.

By the late 1930s, therefore, Britain's commitment to its empire was effectively as strong as it had ever been. In the opinion of one historian, 'imperialism truly came of age in the inter-war years' (August, 1985: 20). To be sure, the upheavals in the international economy and the challenges of colonial nationalism had obliged the British to reconsider the character of their relationship to the constituent elements of their empire. But the outcome of that reconsideration was neither the renunciation of, nor the retreat from, empire. On the contrary, these far-flung imperial possessions came to be seen by Britain's leaders as more valuable than ever as the world slipped into economic autarky and political anarchy, which accounts for their unprecedented efforts to persuade the public of its varied benefits. After 1937, however, the question that came to confront the British was how this imperial system could be sustained in the face of the military adventurism of the fascist states.

CHAPTER SIX

FROM APPEASEMENT TO GLOBAL WAR,
1937–45

It is widely accepted that the period leading up to the Second World War and continuing through to its conclusion presented modern Britain with its greatest challenge as a global power. The outcome would have a profound effect on its subsequent standing in the world, relegating it to a subsidiary role in the Cold War rivalry between the United States and the Soviet Union. Yet much of the literature on the world crisis that brought Britain to this denouement is preoccupied almost entirely with its European dimension, concentrating in particular on the threat from Hitler. Because his actions endangered the very existence of the British state and provoked the popular response that made 'the people's war' a mythic source of national pride, it is understandable that the struggle against Germany has attracted so much attention. Yet this focus has unwittingly obscured the wider array of forces that informed the origins and outcome of this crisis for Britain. More particularly, it has hidden the importance of the empire to the pursuit of appeasement by Neville Chamberlain and the pursuit of victory by his successor, Winston Churchill.

By restoring the empire to its proper place in the story of the British struggle against the fascist states, we gain a richer understanding of the Second World War's significance for Britain itself. It obviously alters the parochial view of the war as a struggle over the sanctity of the home island and an impetus to a new national spirit; it also complicates the popular view of the war as an event that set in motion the forces of decolonisation and the retreat from power. As historians of the British Empire have insisted for some time, the Second World War inspired a renewal of imperial ambition among the British (Gallagher, 1982; Louis, 1978), creating an environment within which 'the imperial idea grew strong in confidence and temper' (Thornton, 1968: 360). And although the costs of the conflict may have been too heavy to take as much advantage of the opportunities it presented as the imperialists would have wished, Britain did emerge from the war victorious and determined to maintain its empire.

THE LOGIC OF APPEASEMENT

Whitehall confronted a nightmare scenario in the late 1930s. The expansionist ambitions of Germany, Japan and Italy had begun to collide with British interests. Any one of these powers would have presented a significant strategic challenge for Britain, which was poorly prepared to counter aggression after more than a decade of military cutbacks and disarmament treaties. But the prospect of going to war against all three of these fascist states was beyond the realm of realistic preparation, as the Committee of Imperial Defence made clear in a 1937 report [*Doc. 24*]. Each of them threatened a different part of Britain and its empire. In 1935 Italy invaded Ethiopia, establishing itself as a rival Mediterranean power and drawing uncomfortably close to the Suez Canal and East Africa. In 1937 Japan renewed its war against China, jeopardising British trade entrepôts at Shanghai and Hong Kong and generating anxiety in Australia and New Zealand. And in 1938 Germany annexed Austria and announced its claims to the Sudetenland in Czechoslovakia, overturning the territorial settlement imposed at Versailles, undermining the framework of peace in Europe, and placing the security of the British Isles itself at risk.

The British responded by pursuing a policy of appeasement. While the massive literature on this subject has shown that the appeasers acted out of a complex mix of motives, what requires highlighting for our purposes is that their perspective on the problem was an imperial one. Though the German threat impinged most directly on the home islands, it was assessed in the context of the other forces that encroached on Britain's global interests. Appeasement was intended above all to find a formula to prevent those forces from combining. The Hoare–Laval plan, for example, sought to placate the Italians by abandoning League of Nations sanctions and recognising their conquest of Ethiopia. Officials also sought ways to satisfy the Japanese, though little came of these discussions. Germany was the main focus of appeasement efforts, both because its expansionist designs seemed most threatening to Britain itself and because it seemed least threatening to British imperial interests. Although the Germans did call for the return of the colonies taken from them at Versailles, their real ambitions were directed eastward towards 'people of whom we know nothing', in Neville Chamberlain's infamous phrase. For Chamberlain and many of his countrymen, the appeasement of German demands in Central Europe was less objectionable than the appeasement of the other two aggressors, whose interests impinged more directly on the British Empire.

Another impetus for the efforts to appease Germany was the unwillingness of the Dominions to lend support to a more forceful position by Britain. This was made clear by Dominion leaders at the Imperial Conference of 1937 and reinforced by their objections to giving guarantees to Czechoslovakia in 1938 [*Doc. 25*]. Although their position may have 'only confirmed Chamberlain on a course of action on which he had already decided', it presented an impediment to any serious consideration of other options. The prospect of the Commonwealth breaking up over the issue of war was a 'decisive' factor in the prime minister's determination to reach a settlement at Munich (Ovendale, 1975: 319).

Appeasement had its opponents, of course, and their stance too was informed in important ways by their attitudes towards the empire. The most prominent critic was Winston Churchill, who viewed the appeasement of Germany in the same light as he had held the 1935 Government of India Act – that is, as evidence of imperial retreat. He had no patience for the government's efforts to reduce the range of challengers arrayed against Britain, insisting instead on an unyielding response to anyone who dared to threaten its imperial interests, whether they came from within the empire or from outside its borders. Other uncompromising imperialists like Lord Lloyd and Lord Birkenhead shared his pugnacity (Charmley, 1993). Their objections to appeasement attracted some strange bedfellows. Communists and many other leftists were ideologically opposed to any accommodation of the fascist states (although the Communist Party of Great Britain reversed itself after the announcement of the Hitler–Stalin Pact in 1939). They regarded the aggressive actions of Germany, Italy and Japan as evidence that fascism was imperialistic by its very nature (Howe, 1993). Left and right came together around the conviction that the appetites of the Axis powers were essentially unappeasable. Their appraisal was in effect affirmed by the outbreak of war in September 1939.

Even though fighting was initially limited to Europe, the British strategy for survival depended in large measure on the resources of the empire. Those resources, however, could not be called forth as readily as they had been at the start of the First World War. The self-governing Dominions in particular were free to make their own decisions about whether to enter the war. It must have given the constitutional architects of the inter-war Commonwealth – what John Darwin has termed the 'Third British Empire' (Darwin, in Brown and Louis, 1999) – a good deal of satisfaction to find their faith in the bonds of race and royalty affirmed by the willingness of all the Dominions except Ireland to declare their allegiance to the British cause. Ironically, appeasement had laid the groundwork for their support through its demonstration that no concessions could prevent a collision with Germany (Ovendale, 1975). New Zealand, ever loyal, went to war with alacrity. So did Australia, understanding that its own security was intimately tied to the fate of Britain. The Canadian decision was delayed a week until its parliament could convene, but the outcome was never in doubt. It *was* in doubt in South Africa, where Prime Minister Hertzog argued for neutrality, but a narrow majority in parliament backed the pro-war stance of Jan Smuts (Mansergh, II, 1982). Only Ireland, which had already effectively removed itself from the Commonwealth in the 1930s under the republican leadership of Eamon de Valera, refused to enter the fray, even though the British dangled an offer to reconsider partition in return for an Irish declaration of war (Boyce, 1996: 98).

The dependent empire enjoyed no such autonomy: its subjects were drawn into the war with much the same authoritarian aplomb the British had exercised in 1914. But this time it became necessary for colonial officials to contend with more restive, politically mobilised populations. The Viceroy's failure to consult Indian leaders before declaring that critical colony's entry into the war outraged nationalists, who interpreted his high-handed action as proof that all the talk about Dominion status was nothing more than an empty promise. Members of the Congress Party resigned *en masse* from their parliamentary and ministerial positions, assuming an increasingly adversarial stance towards the colonial state. In Egypt, the political independence granted under the Anglo-Egyptian Treaty of 1936 went by the wayside as the British re-imposed control over this strategically vital region. Nationalists' objections were crushed under the weight of the massive military force that was garrisoned in their country. Across the empire, the outbreak of hostilities caused colonial states to adopt much more intrusive and autocratic policies, suppressing any political dissent that interfered with the pursuit of victory. For African colonies the war laid the groundwork for what has been called the 'second colonial occupation' of the post-war era (Killingray and Rathbone, 1986: 10). The contrast with the British approach to the Dominions was stark, exposing the authoritarian ethos that undergirded the governance of non-white peoples. The underlying objectives of the British, however, were the same – to make use of imperial manpower, manufacturing and raw materials for the war effort.

RESOURCES AND COMMITMENTS

With the sudden and unexpected collapse of France in June 1940, the British strategy for survival rested on withstanding the German onslaught until the empire's widely dispersed resources could be brought to bear on the conflict. The Second World War saw those resources mobilised 'to an unprecedented degree' (Reynolds, 1991: 164). The empire once again was a vital reservoir of military manpower. The Dominions put some two million men in uniform, including 938,000 Australians, 724,000 Canadians, 205,000 New Zealanders, and 200,000 South Africans. India, however, eclipsed those numbers, mobilising two and a half million men for military service in spite of the nationalist agitation that wracked the subcontinent. To be sure, almost one-third of these forces were needed for domestic security, but others were deployed from Egypt to Hong Kong, demonstrating their continued importance as an imperial constabulary (Perry, 1988). Half a million soldiers were recruited from the African colonies. Some fought in the East and North African campaigns, though most served in non-combatant labour corps as they had done in the First World War (Killingray and Rathbone, 1986).

The empire's economic contributions to the war effort are less easily calculated, but no less significant. The Dominions supplied manufactured goods and agricultural commodities. The biggest boon, however, came from the dependent empire. By 1943 India was producing 'more goods for the war than Australia, New Zealand and South Africa combined' (Gallagher, 1982: 141). Africa assumed increased importance as a source of raw materials after the Japanese overran Britain's East Asian colonies in late 1941 and early 1942. It began to generate unprecedented quantities of the minerals, oils, fibres and foodstuffs needed by wartime Britain. The Colonial Development and Welfare Act of 1940 provided £5 million per annum to colonies for economic and social development, though most of those funds were frozen during the war [*Doc. 26*]. The real impetus for the increased production came from colonial officials, who responded to the crisis by creating command economies, organising production drives, establishing marketing monopolies, imposing price and currency exchange controls, and employing other measures to squeeze more resources from their subjects. While some groups benefited from the war economy, many others suffered. In Africa, officials requisitioned cattle and impressed labour (100,000 for work in the Nigerian tin mines alone), precipitating unrest and famine (Havinden and Meredith, 1993: 207). In India, some three million Bengalis died in a famine brought on in part by the effects of the war economy (Callaghan, 1997: 83). The British were not unappreciative of the human costs of their initiatives, but they acted on the premise that desperate times required desperate measures: accounts would have to be settled after the war was over.

Wartime priorities also shaped the financial relationship between Britain and its colonial subjects. The depression-inspired sterling area came into its own during the war as a mechanism that allowed London to control the sterling surpluses of its colonies, preventing their conversion to dollars and thereby bolstering the pound. These surpluses ballooned as colonies exported more goods to meet Britain's war needs but imported less as the disruptions of war and the closed currency system strangled supply. By 1945 India had amassed £1.3 billion in sterling credits it could not spend (Tomlinson, 1979: 140); some African colonies accumulated significant surpluses as well. An infuriated Churchill could not understand how Britain found itself in debt to India, and this reversal of fortune did hold disturbing implications for the future of the Raj. But the sterling zone 'proved an indispensable contribution to financing the war effort' (Krozewski, 1993:

Plate 1 Sir John Tenniel 'My Boys' (1885): Bursting with imperial pride, the British lion admires his cubs, troops from Canada, Australia and other settler colonies. (Collection of the Library of Congress)

Plate 2   Charles Gibson, 'Egypt and John Bull' (n.d.): Egypt as the seductress Cleopatra, tempting John Bull, the reluctant imperialist. (Collection of the Library of Congress)

EASTWARD HO!

Britannia (to India) "We can ill spare him,—but you see we give you
of our best."

Plate 3 Bernard Partridge, 'Eastward Ho!' (1902): India is a helpless maiden
placed by Britannia under the protective care of Lord Kitchener, the Indian army's
new Commander-in-Chief. (Collection of the Library of Congress)

Plate 4 Frederick Opper, 'Dope! Will John Bull's "Pipe Dream" Ever Come True?'
(1902): This American cartoonist portrays Joseph Chamberlain as an opium dealer
and John Bull as his addicted client, dreaming of victory over the Afrikaners in
South Africa. (Collection of the Library of Congress)

Over his head.

Plate 5 Cesare, 'Over His Head' (1916): The Easter Rising is viewed from the perspective of a British officer in Europe, whose attention turns to the revolutionary explosion behind his back in Ireland. (Collection of the Library of Congress)

ITS A GREAT TRICK - IF HE CAN DO IT

Plate 6 Edwin Marcus, 'It's a Great Trick – If He Can Do It' (1942): Stafford Cripps, the British Cabinet minister sent to India during the war to negotiate with the Congress Party, is portrayed here as a magician attempting to hypnotise the nationalists. (Courtesy of Donald Marcus; Collection of the Library of Congress)

243). Its closed currency kept colonies within Britain's economic orbit, counteracting the gravitational pull of the powerful American economy. And its accumulated surpluses supported the financing of about half of Britain's war deficit, thereby reducing its own economic dependence on the United States through the Lend-Lease programme (Cowen and Westcott, in Killingray and Rathbone, 1986).

While Britain drew substantial resources from the empire, it also shouldered significant obligations. Initially these were concentrated in North Africa and the Middle East in response to the threats posed by the Italians and Germans. But Japan's entry into the war in late 1941 brought into play a vast new array of strategic concerns and commitments, stretching from East Asia down through Southeast Asia to India in the west and Australia and the Pacific Islands to the south and east. The nightmare scenario that appeasement had been intended to forestall was now a reality. Only the concurrent entry of the United States into the conflict saved the British from utter disaster in the Asian Pacific arena. Even so, they confronted the daunting task of conducting a world war that was genuinely world-wide, with fronts along the fault-lines of imperial rivalries in Europe, North Africa, the Middle East, Southeast Asia, East Asia and the Pacific.

THE EMPIRE IN THE BALANCE

The war against Japan held especially profound implications for Britain's future as an imperial power. Colonial officials often made much ado about the importance of prestige – otherwise known as bluff – in sustaining their authority over subject peoples. The fall of the supposedly impregnable naval base at Singapore and the surrender of its 64,000 defenders to a Japanese force half that size in February 1942 was painful proof that this understanding of the colonial relationship combined insight with arrogance. Britain's political and military leaders were in fact well aware of Singapore's vulnerability, but they doubted that the Japanese would have the audacity to expose its unwarranted reputation. Winston Churchill, for example, wrote reassuringly in a 1939 memorandum of 'how vain is the menace that Japan will send a fleet and army to conquer Singapore' (Thorne, 1978: 3). When it did, the British saw their power disintegrate across the entire region. The fact that other Western imperial powers suffered similar fates was cold comfort. The British were both baffled and outraged that an Asian people had managed to sweep them from their throne with such apparent ease. They came to view the war in crudely racialist terms, portraying it as an elemental struggle between the white and yellow races (Thorne, 1978).

The effects of the Japanese onslaught extended far beyond the swath of colonial territories that actually fell to its armies. The core components of Britain's empire in the east – India, Australia and New Zealand – escaped invasion, but the relationship between these states and their imperial master/mother country was fundamentally altered. Some Indians came to view the Japanese as agents of liberation. The prominent nationalist Subhas Chandra Bose assumed leadership of the Japanese-sponsored Indian National Army, which recruited captured Indian troops to fight against the British. Most nationalist leaders, including Gandhi and Nehru, were hostile to the Japanese and the Axis cause, but they were not about to pass up the opportunity the war presented to press the British for political concessions. By 1942 the precariousness of the situation would compel Churchill to send out Sir Stafford Cripps, a socialist Cabinet minister who expressed sympathy for the Indians' struggle for independence, to seek a compromise. He offered Indian leaders self-government within the Commonwealth after the war, but with the proviso that Muslims and others could opt out of a central state. This offer did not go far enough for Gandhi and the Congress Party, who rejected it and launched the 'Quit India' campaign to force the British out of the subcontinent. In its scale and determination, this upheaval proved to be the most serious challenge to British rule since the Indian rebellion of 1857. Although authorities eventually suppressed the insurrection, most observers were left with little doubt that the Raj was near its end.

The war with Japan also undermined Britain's influence on Australia and New Zealand. Both Dominions had put their security in the hands of the British government, accepting assurances that the Royal Navy was prepared to protect them against the Japanese threat. They had even agreed to the deployment of most of their trained troops in the Middle East with the understanding that their own defence would not be jeopardised. The fall of Singapore exposed the emptiness of those promises. The antipodeans' anger at the British for placing them in such a precarious position is aptly summarised in the title of one Australian historian's book on the subject, 'The Great Betrayal' (Day, 1988). The failure to fulfil its defence commitments stripped Britain of the political leverage it had previously enjoyed in its dealings with the two Dominions. Henceforth they would seek shelter under the strategic umbrella of the United States, the only ally capable of providing protection against Japanese expansion.

The United States presented its own paradoxical set of problems for the British Empire. From the start Winston Churchill had recognised that Britain's survival depended on America's entry into the war, and he had worked assiduously to cultivate the American president, Franklin D. Roosevelt. But Roosevelt harboured a deep-seated antagonism to colonial rule, and he clashed with Churchill repeatedly over the fate of the European empires, declaring at one point: 'I can't believe that we can fight the war against fascist slavery, and at the same time not work to free people all over the world from a backward colonial policy' (Louis, 1978: 121). When the two leaders met to draft the Atlantic Charter (1941), a declaration of the political ideals informing the allied cause, Roosevelt insisted that it include the famous Article 3, which declared 'the right of all peoples to choose the form of government under which they live'. Churchill sought to interpret the statement as referring only to fascism's European victims, but colonial subjects around the globe were quick to seize on it to bolster their claims for independence. American pressure on the British to loosen their imperial grasp was one of the reasons that the two powers were, in the words of one historian, 'allies of a kind', whose aims often clashed (Thorne, 1978). Indeed, so tense did their relationship become that some of Britain's political leaders came to regard the United States as nearly as threatening to the future of British power as their common enemy, the Axis powers (Charmley, 1993).

It would be a mistake, however, to assume that the British were thrown entirely on the defence in their efforts to keep the empire whole. They also saw the war as an opportunity to strengthen and expand their imperial holdings, much as they had done in the First World War. At least in the short term, their position in sub-Saharan Africa was strengthened by the war, which substantially enhanced colonial authorities' ability to shape the social and economic lives of their subjects. British officials dusted off federation plans for East and Central Africa in anticipation that the subcontinent could be turned into a new and improved India, operating under the civilising supervision of white settlers. They had little trouble convincing American officials who harboured their own racial prejudices against blacks that Africans could not be trusted to govern themselves for the foreseeable future.

In North Africa and the Middle East, British imperial ambitions also enjoyed something of a revival. Not only did they reassert control over states such as Egypt and Iraq, which were already recognised to be within their sphere of influence; they also extended their reach into neighbouring areas that had been under French and Italian control, and imposed themselves once again on Persia, an object of their attentions since the First World War. They contemplated a scheme to acquire post-war trusteeships over the ex-Italian colonies in North and East Africa and, despite (or perhaps because of) the problems that Jewish immigration caused them in Palestine, they bandied about the idea of creating a satellite colony for Jews in Libya (Louis, 1978).

Even in Asia the British did not consider the situation unrecoverable. They remained convinced that after the war they could restore their rule over the colonies conquered by Japan. And so they did in Malaya, Singapore, Hong Kong, and elsewhere; only the Burmese proved implacably opposed to their return. Not even India was written off as lost, least of all by Churchill, who adamantly – and many of his colleagues thought irrationally – resisted any concessions to nationalists. Leo Amery, who served as Secretary of State for India in the war government, adopted the more conventional view that Indian independence was inevitable, but that this need not mean the severance of its bonds to Britain: if India could be persuaded to accept membership in the Commonwealth, there was reason to hope for the survival of the imperial relationship in modified form (Louis, 1992).

In the end, even the Americans were brought round to a more accommodating attitude towards the British Empire. This was due in part to the success of the British in casting their colonial practices in a humanitarian rhetoric of trusteeship, which went over well with the Americans. This rhetoric was reinforced by policy initiatives, the most notable being the Colonial Development and Welfare Act of 1945, which increased the pool of aid money from £5 to £12 million per annum and directed more of it to health and social services (Havinden and Meredith, 1993). The British case for colonies also benefited from shifts in the strategic situation during the latter stages of the war. The Americans' military success in the Pacific began to give rise to imperial ambitions of their own, weakening the moral weight of their case against the British Empire. And the Soviet Union began to position itself as the West's great post-war rival, placing the future of the colonial world in a new strategic context. By 1945 the United States had backed away from its earlier objections to European colonialism and adopted a policy far more friendly to British imperial interests (Louis, 1978).

BRINGING THE EMPIRE HOME

The British domestic scene during the Second World War bore a number of similarities to its predecessor in the previous world war. Once again regular politics were suspended as the major parties joined together in a coalition government. Once again the state assumed far-reaching powers over production, prices, wages and other aspects of economic and social life. Once again the demands of total war brought in its train significant repercussions for class, gender and race relations. And yet the influence of the war on the relationship between Britain and its empire is not as transparent as was the case for the First World War.

With Winston Churchill as prime minister, the wartime government's commitment to the empire was unshakeable. 'I have not become the King's First Minister', he famously declared in 1942, 'in order to preside over the liquidation of the British Empire' (Louis, 1978: 200). This was a view he reiterated time and again [*Doc. 27*]. He wielded so much personal power over the conduct of British foreign policy that no one could mistake this statement for mere bluster. But unlike David Lloyd George, his First World

War counterpart, he lacked any interest in or appreciation for the ways in which an imperial foreign policy could be connected to a social imperial policy at home. It was this fact above all that frustrated Leo Amery, causing him to grumble about Churchill's failure to grasp the opportunities the war presented. Even though Amery himself was a member of the War Cabinet, he operated in a far less hospitable environment than did his mentor, Milner, and the other social imperialists who dominated the government during the First World War. This was not only owing to Churchill's lack of interest, but to the influence of the Labour ministers, who enjoyed a remarkably free hand in determining the direction of home affairs. As post-war events would show, Labour leaders were no less determined than their Conservative rivals to maintain Britain's standing as a great imperial power, but they did not share the social imperialists' conviction that this agenda should be carried over into the domestic sphere. There was no imperial dimension to the Beveridge Report (1942), the key domestic policy statement of the war years, which prepared the way for what became known as the welfare state, with its recommendations regarding social services for all citizens 'from the cradle to the grave'. The enthusiastic public reaction to this report strengthened the hands of Labour and restrained the social imperialists from marshalling the wartime powers of the state towards their own ends.

In the public realm, however, there is little indication that the empire diminished in popularity during the war. Although the subject remains under-researched, there is evidence that the war generated an 'outburst of patriotic and imperial fervour' among the British people (MacKenzie, 1984: 234). The fact that most of the fighting until 1944 occurred outside Europe in defence of places like Egypt, Singapore and India gave the war a distinctly imperial cast both for the troops stationed there and for their loved ones at home. Movies with imperial themes were as popular as ever. The Empire Day Movement enjoyed unprecedented support. The Imperial Institute found a renewed sense of purpose, launching an aggressive campaign that extolled the virtues of empire in lectures, films and literature. The Ministry of Information and the BBC turned much of their energies to imperial propaganda as well.

The war also brought the empire home to many Britons in an increasingly visceral way. Once again, the labour demands of total war compelled authorities to recruit colonial workers. A thousand Honduran foresters were sent to the Edinburgh area for war work and 350 West Indian technicians were imported to Merseyside. Some two-thirds of the black Caribbean immigrants who arrived in Britain after the war on the *Empire Windrush*, the ship that symbolised the ushering in of a new multiracial era, were returning to the land where they had been stationed for war service (Spencer, 1995: 213). When the Royal Navy's demand for skilled British sailors created a shortage of merchant seamen, the government revoked the Special Restriction (Coloured Alien Seamen) Order of 1925, opening the door once again to the use of South Asian lascars on British vessels – and the growth of South Asian communities in British cities (Holmes, 1988). More Britons than ever before came into personal contact with peoples whose skin colour and customs differed from their own. In addition to South Asians and West Indians, some 130,000 black American GIs were stationed in Britain in the latter part of the war. Though many Britons were appalled by the racism shown towards these troops by their white American counterparts, others shared these prejudices, and they came to the fore with particular fervour when black GIs fraternised with British women (Reynolds, 1995). Once again the intersection of race and sex stirred strong emotions and stern warnings, much as it had done during the First World War: the 'good-time' girls who associated with black men became the targets of moral censure, which condemned their behaviour for undermining the nation's unity and virtue (Rose, 1998). The more telling point, however, is that the war made racial encounters much more a part of the everyday experience of the British public. As one historian of the subject has noted, 'the war was a watershed in the formation of the specific ethnic and cultural character of multiracial Britain that developed in the last half of the twentieth century' (Spencer, 1995: 209).

When the war came to an end in 1945, Britain was indisputably a different country from what it had been in 1939. Not only was it a more ethnically diverse country than before the war, and one poised to become even more so; it was also a country whose citizens had acquired in the course of the conflict a more powerful and binding sense of national pride, forged from adversity and framed in ways that revisited what it meant to be British. It remained to be seen whether these two developments would accommodate themselves to one another or collide: the post-war debates about the rights of citizenship centred on precisely this issue. It also remained to be seen how Britain would respond to the unprecedented array of challenges that confronted it in the aftermath of the war. Much of its manufacturing infrastructure was shattered, its merchant fleet under the sea, its export economy in disarray, its overseas assets sold off. Its war debts totalled £4.7 billion (Reynolds, 1991: 159). Its ability to influence affairs in the international arena was reduced, its power undeniably diminished.

What implications the war's transformations had on Britain's relationship to its empire is the subject of sharp dispute. Some historians share the opinion of a wartime minister who asserted in 1943 that the Second World War was 'the last brilliant flare-up which illuminates the darkness of the decline of British power and influence' (Charmley, 1993: 571; see also Barnett, 1972). If the empire was coterminous with global power, then it is difficult to refute the claim that the war was imperial Britain's death knell.

But the association between the one and the other is perhaps less direct than we might assume. Much of the scholarship on British foreign policy in the post-Second World War era demonstrates that its architects, both Labour and Conservative, were determined to maintain the empire in the face of an evident diminution of national power. As one recent survey of research on the subject declares, 'the empire took on a new significance for Britain in the post-war world' (White, 1999: 6) – though it might be asked whether it was really 'new' or simply renewed. The immediate post-war years are of course beyond the scope of this study, but it is relevant to our concerns to note that those who shaped British policy in this period did not automatically resign themselves to the view that the deterioration of their country's international influence was irrevocable or that it necessitated the wholesale abandonment of empire.

Whatever the costs of the Second World War, it is doubtful that the commitment to empire was one of them. This global struggle brought every corner of the British Empire into play, and although it exposed and exacerbated the problems that confronted the architects of imperial defence, it also demonstrated the degree to which the empire had become an integral part of the British state and its citizens' sense of self. Economically, politically, militarily and emotionally, Britain's efforts to stave off the challenges of its enemies were framed in terms of its imperial interests and identity.

PART THREE ASSESSMENT

CHAPTER SEVEN

CONCLUSIONS

The purpose of this book has been to provide an introduction to the imperial history of Britain in the period 1880–1945. It is worth noting that an imperial history of Britain is not a history of the British Empire, nor is it a history of the British Isles; it is instead a history of the intersections of these two dimensions of the British experience, which are too often viewed apart from one another. After 1880, a broad range of forces brought Britain's domestic realm into closer association with its imperial arena. The preceding chapters have sought to identify some of these forces and consider their impact on Britain, its people, and their place in the world.

Two sets of relationships are central to the issues raised in this study. One is the relationship between empire and the projection of British power; the other is the relationship between empire and the properties of the British nation-state. In neither case was the relationship as simple or straightforward as might be supposed.

Although there is an obvious association between empire and power, the relative increase in global power does not necessarily manifest itself in imperial expansion, nor does its diminishment necessarily result in imperial retreat. The distinction is an important one for making sense of the British experience, even though it runs contrary to the assumptions of the imperialists themselves, as well as those of certain scholars. There is little doubt that the power the British wielded abroad – whether measured in economic or political or military terms – declined relative to rival states after about 1880, and despite occasional pauses it continued its slide through much of the twentieth century. The British Empire, however, experienced its greatest period of expansion in the late nineteenth century, followed by another push forward in the aftermath of the First World War. It suffered no serious territorial setbacks until the Japanese conquest of its East Asian possessions in 1942, and those losses were reversed by 1945. When British power was most obviously under duress, British imperialism was most obviously engaged in aggressive action. Thus, the expansionist ambitions of other European states in the late nineteenth century stirred Britain to assert claims to vast tracts of Africa and other overseas territories; the crisis caused by the South African War threw it into a frenzied effort to shore up imperial security and shape up an imperial 'race'; the upheaval of the First World War cleared the way and roused the appetite for a major new round of imperial expansion; even the Second World War, which proved so destructive to Britain's position as a great power, inspired a renewed imperial purpose that translated into the temporary consolidation of the empire in Africa and the Middle East. All arguments that seek to draw a direct correlation between the ebbs and flows of British power and those of the British Empire are bound to be frustrated by the fact that the former is measured in relative terms while the latter is not.

A similar problem afflicts arguments that reverse the dynamics of the relationship by attributing the deterioration of British power to an unhealthy dependence on the British Empire. While evidence can be marshalled to show that some businessmen turned to the empire for refuge from economic competition, just as some statesmen figured it into their decision to appease fascist aggressors, it is not clear how Britain's international position would have improved in the absence of its empire. Despite the urgings of Joseph Chamberlain and others, the British never retreated into imperial autarky: the closest they came was when the international economy collapsed in the depression of the 1930s, leaving imperial preference almost the only option available for keeping their export trade alive. Nor did the empire provide the British with any incentive to pursue a policy of political isolationism. On the contrary, it can be argued that it was precisely because the interests of the empire impinged on so many parts of the world that Britain was so actively and continuously engaged in the global system, the main arena within which competing states tested their relative power. Once again we are left to conclude that the British Empire was associated with British power, but not in such a way that either one had a direct causal effect on the other.

The relationship between the empire and the British nation-state also is susceptible to misperceptions, though they tend to be the inverse of those affecting our understanding of empire and British power. Here the problem is not the unwarranted effort to couple two distinct if related phenomena, but an equally unwarranted reluctance to recognise that two seemingly separate phenomena were in fact connected to one another. Empires and nations tend to be viewed as distinct and deeply antagonistic strategies for structuring states and mobilising peoples. But this does not accord with the British experience in the period examined in this book. What appears so striking about that experience is that it blurred the boundaries between the nation and the empire both at the ideological and the institutional levels, establishing the lineaments of an imperial nationalism and an imperial state.

The ideological dimensions of this integrative endeavour operated at various levels and affected various constituencies. Social Darwinism, national 'efficiency', imperial preference, and other doctrines and proposals created a yeasty ferment that intoxicated political and intellectual elites with the proposition that the nation's fate somehow hinged on its imperial presence. Particular imperial policies were promoted by a whole host of voluntary associations, ranging from philanthropic societies that encouraged empire migration to business lobbies that pressed for tariff reform to service organisations that advocated imperial defence. The music halls' jingoistic assertions of national pride and the popular press's sensationalist coverage of colonial wars inspired imperial patriotism among the late-Victorian and Edwardian publics, while radio and the cinema provided powerful new media through which a similar spirit spread to the inter-war generation. Trade exhibitions, museum displays and royal events offered 'spectacles of empire' that excited and informed audiences. The history and geography curriculum taught in the schools, the adventure stories published in boys' magazines, and the ethos and activities of groups like the Boy Scouts raised the imperial consciousness of the young. Women asserted their own claims of contribution to the imperial enterprise through their involvement in philanthropic and political organisations that promoted emigration to the colonies and intervention in indigenous gender practices. Nor was this ideological advocacy of empire limited to those who assumed the privileged perspective of British shores. Many of the Dominions' inhabitants shared this sense of commitment to the imperial cause, regarding themselves as members of a Greater Britain. More surprisingly, perhaps, so too did some of the dependent colonies' Western-educated elites, at least in a provisional way before events turned them against the empire. Powerful forces worked to erode the distinctions between a national and an imperial identity.

These same forces sought to build institutional bridges between the nation and the empire. Some of these bridges never made it past the blue-print stage: the chimera of an imperial parliament tempted several generations of imperial idealists into arid debates about its constitutional design. Other efforts to engineer imperial bonds were realised, but failed to fulfil the expectations of their architects: this clearly was the case for the version of imperial preference implemented at the Ottawa Conference. Similar charges can be lodged against other initiatives that sought closer institutional ties between the nation and the empire: few of them fully measured up to their promise. But neither were they negligible. Though the Statute of Westminster was woven from the gossamer threads of royalty and 'race' patriotism, for example, it managed to make the Commonwealth a surprisingly cohesive – and enduring – imperial fraternity. Many of the policies and programmes that promoted the imperial connection arose over time as Britain's altered circumstances dictated new and more aggressive strategies. Efforts to steer emigrants in an imperial direction evolved from the Emigrants' Information Office's promotional activities before the First World War through the schemes to settle ex-servicemen in the colonies immediately after the war to the Empire Settlement Act's financing of various migration initiatives between the wars, in each case acting in collaboration with the emigration activities of private societies. Efforts to stimulate trade between Britain and its colonies reflected the deterioration of its standing in the international economy as the free trade policies of the pre-war years gave way to the state-directed initiatives of the inter-war years, ranging from the Empire Marketing Board to the Ottawa agreement and the Colonial Development Acts to the sterling area. And efforts to strengthen the security of the nation took on an increasingly imperial colour as the threats arrayed against Britain obliged it to calculate both its commitments and its resources in terms of the empire, with the Committee of Imperial Defence the earliest institutionalised expression of this appreciation that any outbreak of hostilities against rival powers would almost inevitably assume imperial – and hence global – dimensions. Both world wars confirmed this analysis.

Perhaps the most sustained and effective effort to connect the British public to the empire was social imperialism. This potent mixture of imperial patriotism and social reform was a strategic move undertaken in response to the rising power of the newly enfranchised masses, whom it was felt could only be contained by investing them with a sense of civic responsibility. This was the intent of social imperialism. It sought to cultivate the masses' loyalties to the state by making them both the beneficiaries of new social services and the bearers of new social obligations, and it sought to structure those services and obligations in such a way that the empire came to be seen as an integral part of the state. This ambitious undertaking brought together figures from across the political spectrum, turning antagonists like Lloyd George and Lord Curzon into allies. Though social imperialism reached the height of its influence in the period between the end of the South African War and the end of the First World War, it continued to inform state policies and political perspectives through the inter-war years and beyond.

The empire was so entangled in the British experience during the period surveyed by this volume that it is in certain respects beside the point to differentiate imperial influences from domestic ones. The real task instead is to demonstrate how far imperial influences became an integral element of British identity and institutions. By way of example it is worth considering what it meant to be an imperialist in this era. No one was more self-consciously supportive of the empire than Joseph Chamberlain and his fellow advocates of imperial protectionism – no one, that is, except for Winston Churchill and other free traders of the same stripe. Conservative

Unionists claimed proprietary rights to imperial patriotism, but that radical 'pro-Boer' Liberal, David Lloyd George, did more than any prime minister in the twentieth century to expand the empire's reach. Among the strongest advocates of social imperialism were the Tory nationalist Lord Milner *and* the Fabian socialist Sidney Webb. It is no more surprising that Webb served as Colonial Secretary in the second Labour government than that Milner did so in the Lloyd George coalition. Labour Party leaders were determined to conduct imperial business as usual. Even principled critics like E. D. Morel and J. A. Hobson objected less to the fact that their country had colonies than to the way it ran them. In short, nearly everyone was implicated in the empire in one way or another. It permeated all aspects of British life, colouring attitudes and actions at the political, economic, social, intellectual, and even emotional levels. Its size, diversity and importance allowed it to assume different meanings for different people, eluding efforts to confine it through association with a particular policy or doctrine. It is precisely this combination of elusiveness and pervasiveness that made it such a powerful part of the modern British experience.

The British fought innumerable small wars in the late nineteenth century against native peoples who resisted their expansionist ambitions in Africa and Asia. The lessons the military learned in these clashes are noted in this excerpt from a classic study of guerrilla warfare, written by an officer who participated in several colonial campaigns.

... [G]uerilla warfare is a form of operation above all things to be avoided. The whole spirit of the art of conducting small wars is to strive for the attainment of decisive methods, the very essence of partisan warfare from the point of the enemy being to avoid definite engagements. The inconveniences and dangers to regular troops when the adversary adopts this attitude are fully recognised by competent commanders. But no amount of energy and strategic skill will at times draw the enemy into risking engagements, or induce him to depart from the form of warfare in which most irregular warriors excel and in which regular troops are almost invariably seen at their worst. ... The suppression of the rebellion in Southern Rhodesia in 1896 affords an admirable illustration of the right method of dealing with guerilla warriors of a certain type. ... The scattered impis of the Matabili were hunted down relentlessly and compelled to fight or to submit. ... During the final operations against the Mashonas, it was found that the only way of compelling their submission was to hunt them into their cave strongholds, destroy their kraals, and finally capture them in their caves – a by no means easy task.

Colonel C. E. Callwell, *Small Wars: Their Principles and Practice*, 3rd edn (London: His Majesty's Stationery Office, 1906), pp. 125, 137, 138.

In 1877 Cecil Rhodes, who had just begun to make his fortune in the Kimberley diamond fields of South Africa, drafted a 'confession of faith' that expressed his messianic imperial vision, which held that it was right and proper for the 'Anglo-Saxon race' to expand at the expense of inferior peoples.

I contend that we are the finest race in the world and that the more of the world we inhabit the better it is for the human race. Just fancy those parts that are at present inhabited by the most despicable specimens of human beings what an alternation there would be if they were brought under Anglo-Saxon influence, look again at the extra employment a new country added to our dominions gives [*sic*]. I contend that every acre added to our territory means in the future birth to some more of the English race who otherwise would not be brought into existence. ... Africa is still lying ready for us it is our duty to take it. It is our duty to seize every opportunity of acquiring more territory and we should keep this one idea steadily before our eyes that more territory simply means more of the Anglo-Saxon race more of the best the most human, most honourable race the world possesses [*sic*].

> Cecil Rhodes, 'Confession of Faith', 1877, appendix to John Flint, *Cecil Rhodes* (Boston, MA: Little, Brown, and Co., 1974), pp. 248–9, 250.

DOCUMENT 3   THE IMPERIAL ADVENTURE STORY

Most of G. A. Henty's popular adventure novels for boys were loosely based on historical events on the colonial frontier. The Young Colonist concerns the British struggle against Zulus and Afrikaners in South Africa.

... Looking round they saw a large number of natives crowning the low hills all round them, and saw that while they had been stalking the deer they themselves had been stalked by the natives. ... The arrows were falling fast among them, but none had been hit, and as soon as the preparations were complete they opened a steady fire at the enemy. With the exception of the man who had come out with the horses all were good shots, and their steady fire at once checked the advance of the natives, whose triumphant yelling ceased, as man after man went down.

> G. A. Henty, *The Young Colonists* (New York: Hurst and Co., no date), pp. 165–6.

DOCUMENT 4   SOCIAL DARWINISM

The late-Victorian social theorist Benjamin Kidd sought to explain the expansion of the 'Anglo-Saxon' across the globe in terms of Darwinian science, to which he attributed a natural law of progress that overrode humanitarian concerns for the fate of 'weaker races'.

We watch the Anglo-Saxon overflowing his boundaries, going forth to take possession of new territories, and establishing himself like his ancestors in many lands. A peculiar interest attaches to the sight. He has been deeply affected, more deeply than many others, by the altruistic influences of the ethical system upon which our Western Civilisation is founded. He had seen races like the ancient Peruvians, the Aztecs, and the Caribs, in large part exterminated by others, ruthlessly driven out of existence by the more vigorous invader, and he has at least the wish to do better. ... Yet neither wish nor intention has power apparently to arrest a destiny which works itself out irresistibly. The Anglo-Saxon has exterminated the less developed peoples with which he has come into competition even more effectively than other races have done in like case; not necessarily indeed by fierce and cruel wars of extermination, but through the operation of laws not less deadly and even more certain in their result. The weaker races disappear before the stronger through the effects of mere contact. ... No motives appear to be able to stay the progress of such movements, humanize them how we may. We often in a self-accusing spirit attribute the gradual disappearance of aboriginal peoples to the effects of our vices upon them; but the truth is that what may be called the virtues of our civilisation are scarcely less fatal than its vices. ... Wherever a superior race comes into close contact and competition with an inferior race, the result seems to be much the same, whether it is arrived at by the rude method of wars of conquest, or by the silent process which we see at work in Australia, New Zealand, and the North American Continent. ...

Benjamin Kidd, *Social Evolution* (New York: Macmillan, 1894), pp. 45–8.

DOCUMENT 5 SOCIAL INVESTIGATION AS IMPERIAL EXPLORATION

The urban poor came to be seen by many social reformers as the domestic counterparts to the primitive peoples that Stanley and other explorers reported encountering in Africa. The Salvation Army's General Booth makes explicit and sustained use of this analogy in his call for action against poverty in Britain.

As there is a darkest Africa is there not also a darkest England? Civilisation, which can breed its own barbarians, does it not also breed its own pygmies? May we not find a parallel at our own doors, and discover within a stone's throw of our cathedrals and palaces similar horrors to those which Stanley has found existing in the great Equatorial forest? The more the mind dwells upon the subject, the closer the analogy appears. The ivory raiders who brutally traffic in the unfortunate denizens of the forest glades, what are they but the publicans who flourish on the weakness of our poor? The two tribes of savages, the human baboon and the handsome dwarf ... may be accepted as the two varieties who are continually present with us – the vicious, lazy lout, and the toiling slave. ... And just as Mr. Stanley's Zanzibaris lost faith, and could only be induced to plod on in brooding sullenness of dull despair, so the most of our social reformers ... soon become depressed and despairing. ... Who can hope to make headway against the innumerable adverse conditions which doom the dweller in Darkest England to eternal and immutable misery?... The stony streets of

London, if they could but speak, would tell of tragedies as awful, of ruin as complete, of ravishments as horrible, as if we were in Central Africa; only the ghastly devastation is covered, corpse-like, with the artificialities and hypocrisies of modern civilisation.

General William Booth, *In Darkest England and the Way Out* (London: Salvation Army, 1890), pp. 11–13.

DOCUMENT 6   **PRAISING THE BRITISH SOLDIER**

The late nineteenth century saw the public acquire a new respect and appreciation for the common British soldier or 'Tommy', who had until then been widely regarded as a ruffian drawn from the dregs of society. No one did more to raise the reputation of the 'Tommy' than Rudyard Kipling, who wrote an affectionate series of 'barrack room ballads' about the everyday world of the infantryman in India. Here he adopts the voice – and dialect – of a 'Tommy' to chide the British public for their disdain of the men who defend them.

You talk o' better food for us, an' schools, an' fires, an' all:
We'll wait for extry rations if you treat us rational.
Don't mess about the cook-room slops, but prove it to our face
The Widow's Uniform is not the soldier-man's disgrace.
For it's Tommy this, an' Tommy that, an' 'Chuck him out, the brute!'
But it's 'Saviour of 'is country' when the guns begin to shoot;
An' it's Tommy this, an' Tommy that, an' anything you please;
An' Tommy ain't a bloomin' fool – you bet that Tommy sees!

Rudyard Kipling, 'Tommy', in *Rudyard Kipling's Verse: Definitive Edition* (New York: Doubleday, 1952), pp. 397–8.

DOCUMENT 7   **THE RADICAL CRITIQUE OF THE SOUTH AFRICAN WAR**

Some of the most vigorous criticisms of the war came from the British labour movement, which suspected collusion between the British government and capitalists and sympathised with the Afrikaners as underdogs. The great Scottish labour leader, Keir Hardie, voices these views in the following passage.

The war is a capitalists' war, begotten by capitalists' money, lied into being by a perjured mercenary capitalist press, and fathered by unscrupulous politicians, themselves the merest tools of the capitalists. As a pastoral people the Boers doubtless have all the failings of the fine qualities which pertain to that mode of life; but whatever these failings might have been they are virtues compared to the turbid pollution and refined cruelty which is inseparable from the operation of capitalism. As Socialists, our sympathies are bound to be with the Boers. Their Republican form of Government bespeaks freedom, and is thus hateful to tyrants, whilst their methods of production for use are much nearer our ideal than any form of exploitation for profit.

J. Keir Hardie, 'Capitalist's War', *The Labour Leader* (6 January 1900), reprinted in Stephen Koss (ed.), *The Pro-Boers: The Anatomy of an Antiwar Movement* (Chicago, IL: University of Chicago Press, 1973), p. 54.

DOCUMENT 8   THE DIPLOMATIC UPHEAVAL

Here Lord Salisbury considers whether the agreements with Japan and France mark a break with Britain's traditional foreign policy. His conclusion is characteristically cautious, drawing a distinction between the intentions of the two agreements. Note the stress he places on the desire to resolve 'conflicting claims' with France and Germany.

Lansdowne's speech on Tuesday was a most important one. He declared in effect that we had abandoned the policy of isolation, not only in Asia but also in Europe: that we must do as other Powers do, who are distributed in groups: that the Japan treaty and the French agreement have carried this change of policy into effect: and he almost treated these two instruments, though no doubt different in form, as substantially similar. All this is, of course, largely true, but I should be inclined to take some exception to the last. Circumstances no doubt have driven us in respect to France further than we intended. There can be no doubt that originally French policy was wholly different from the Japanese. The latter, on the face of it, though defensive only, was essentially military. The former had its sanction and was intended to have its sanction in diplomatic measures alone. In truth the French agreement was in its inception not a departure from our previous foreign policy, but strictly in accordance with it. For the last twenty years we have been engaged with different Powers, notably with Germany and with France, in adjusting conflicting claims, and in bargaining so as to get rid of causes of friction and if I spoke about our agreement with France, I should treat it rather as a development of past policy than as a new departure.

Lord Salisbury to Arthur Balfour, 9 November 1905, British Library Add. Mss 48758, reproduced in C. J. Lowe, *The Reluctant Imperialists* (London: Routledge and Kegan Paul, 1967), p. 409.

DOCUMENT 9   FEMINISM AND IMPERIALISM

This statement shows how some Edwardian feminists used the belief in racial superiority (and the fear of racial degeneration) to argue the case for extending greater rights to Englishwomen.

It is no exaggeration to say that on woman depends the welfare of the race. ... The endowments of men and women, moral and intellectual, as well as physical, are to a very large extent similar, and with the exception of their absolute sexual characteristics there is more similarity between the male and female of the same race than there is between the males and females of alien races. That is to say, there is more similarity of physical characteristics and of mental and moral endowments between an Englishman and an Englishwoman of the same stage of development than there is between an educated Englishman and a Bantu or Hottentot man.

Mary Scharlieb, *Womanhood and Race-Regeneration* (New York: Moffat, Yard, 1912), pp. 5, 43.

DOCUMENT 10   TARIFF REFORM

Tariff reform took on the character of a crusade for Joseph Chamberlain, who relentlessly pursued the issue until a stroke incapacitated him. His case to the British public spoke both to their fear of economic decline and their sense of imperial pride by arguing that autarky would reduce the former and strengthen the latter.

Ladies and Gentlemen, I feel deeply sensible that the argument I have addressed to you is one of those which will be described by the leader of the Opposition as a squalid argument. A squalid argument! I have appealed to your interests, I have come here as a man of business, I have appealed to the employers and the employed alike in this great city. I have endeavoured to point out to them that their trade, their wages, all depend on the maintenance of this colonial trade, of which some of my opponents speak with such contempt, and, above all, with such egregious ignorance. But now I abandon that line of argument for the moment, and appeal to something higher, which I believe is in your hearts as it is in mine. I appeal to you as fellow citizens of the greatest Empire that the world has ever known; I appeal to you to recognise that the privileges of the Empire bring with them great responsibilities. I want to ask you to think what this Empire means, what it is to you and your descendants. ... [H]ere we have an Empire which with decent organisation and consolidation might be absolutely self-sustaining. Nothing of the kind has ever been known before. There is no article of your food, there is no raw material of your trade, there is no necessity of your lives, no luxury of your existence which cannot be produced somewhere or other in the British Empire, if the British Empire holds together, and if we who have inherited it are worthy of our opportunities. ... I say to you that all that is best in our present life, best in this Britain of ours, all of which we have the right to be most proud, is due to the fact that we are not only sons of Britain, but we are sons of Empire.

Joseph Chamberlain, speech made on 6 October 1903, reprinted in Charles W. Boyd (ed.), *Mr. Chamberlain's Speeches*, Vol. II (London: Constable and Co., 1914), pp. 153–4.

DOCUMENT 11   JINGOISM

The term 'jingoism' entered the vocabulary of political debate in the late nineteenth century to describe popular enthusiasm for colonial wars and other aggressive assertions of national power. Liberal critics like J. A. Hobson believed the music halls and the press manipulated the patriotic emotions of the public and corrupted the democratic process.

The quick ebullition of national hate termed Jingoism is a particular form of this primitive passion, modified and intensified by certain conditions of modern civilisation. ... Among large sections of the middle and labouring classes, the music-hall, and the recreative public-house into which it shades off by imperceptible degrees, are a more potent educator than the church, the school, the political meeting, or even than the press. Into this 'lighter self' of the city populace the artiste conveys by song and recitation crude notions upon morals and politics, appealing by coarse humour or exaggerated pathos to the animal lusts of an audience stimulated by alcohol into appreciative hilarity. In ordinary times politics plays no important part in these feasts of sensationalism, but the glorification of brute force and an ignorant contempt for foreigners are ever-present factors which at great political crises make the music-hall a very serviceable engine for generating military passion.

J. A. Hobson, *The Psychology of Jingoism* (London: Grant Richards, 1901), pp. 2–3.

DOCUMENT 12   WAR PROPAGANDA AND INDIAN LOYALTIES

The British were well aware of German efforts to encourage an Indian uprising during the war. Sir Mancherjee Bhownaggree, a Parsi from Bombay who had moved to England and won election as a Conservative member of Parliament before the war, responds in this propaganda pamphlet, defending Britain against charges of colonial oppression and insisting that Indians are united in their loyalty to the British cause.

One of the methods by which Germany has indulged her hatred of the

British nation is by roundly accusing it of having grossly misgoverned India. To justify that accusation, propagandist literature has been widely distributed in all quarters of the globe by German official writers during the last two years. The people of India have laughed to scorn this grotesque attempt. ... [H]ow ridiculous seem the efforts of the German official propagandists to accuse the British of having misgoverned them, in the hope of alienating their allegiance. It ill becomes a nation whose agents have massacred in cold blood and extirpated the tribe of Herreros ... to talk of the oppression and failure of British rule. ... The people of India have seen through and through the motives of the diabolical propaganda, and they scout the foul charges, the proof or disproof of which must depend on their own verdict. That Verdict is that the destinies of their country have been directed in the paths of progress and prosperity by the government which British genius and British statesmanship have established in India, that they are proud of being British citizens, and that it is only by the right and title of that citizenship that they hope to revive the ancient glory of their mother-land, taking their proper place in the Comity of Nations side by side with the other children of the British Empire.

Sir Mancherjee M. Bhownaggree, *The Verdict of India* (London: Hodder and Stoughton, 1916), foreword, pp. 50–1.

DOCUMENT 13   COLONIAL PEOPLES AND THE MARTIAL SPIRIT

David Lloyd George acknowledges in his War Memoirs *the contributions that Africans, Indians and other colonial peoples made to the British war effort, but he does so in a way that is shot through with racialist assumptions about the roles they were innately suited – and unsuited – to fill.*

In addition to India's great contingent, we drew combatants from the coloured races in our colonies and dependencies of Africa and the West Indies – mainly for service against Germany's African colonies, and in Egypt, Palestine and Mesopotamia – and we recruited from among them numbers of labour battalions for the work of transport, supply and construction along the Western Front. Their toil alone enabled us to throw up with such speed new defences and fresh roads and railways in lieu of those we were forced to abandon in the great retreat of 1918. ... It is true that the total forces supplied to the War by India bore only a trivial proportion of her population – less than the half of one per cent. But most of that population is unwarlike. Their physique unfits them for the nervous and bodily strain of modern war. The chill and dismal humidity of that section of the European battlefield, where the main British forces were massed, proved unsuitable for Indian troops. The fighting races, however, gave us some magnificent troops, who proved their valour and endurance on every front and won a long array of official honours and recognitions. ... The chief contribution of Hindustan was made in southern theatres – Palestine, Mesopotamia and East Africa, where our Indian legions rendered splendid service.

David Lloyd George, War Memoirs: 1918 (Boston: Little, Brown, 1937), pp. 320, 322.

DOCUMENT 14 ARAB NATIONALISM AND THE PARTITION OF THE MIDDLE EAST

The following memorandum, sent to Foreign Secretary Curzon by a British military official in Cairo, points to the sense of betrayal felt by many Arabs after the war as the allies' imperial intentions in the region became clear.

Public opinion throughout Syria and Palestine is united in opposition to any arbitrary division of what they hold to be Arab Territories, and if the issues are decided before they have had an opportunity of stating their case they will regard it as a complete negation of – (A) Principles initiated in the Covenant of the League of Nations.

(B) The principle of the self-determination of peoples so often upheld by the leading Statesmen of the Allied and Associate Powers.

(C) The specific declaration made by Great Britain and France in November 1918.

The present unsettled and anxious state of Moslem opinion throughout the world, owing to the approaching dissolution of the Caliphate, is already being exploited by interested agitators and intriguers throughout the Middle East. Although local political problems occupy the most prominent position at present in the minds of the inhabitants of the various areas, disappointment and disillusionment will render them still more accessible to enemy propaganda and violent local disturbances may combine into a general Anti-Christian and Anti-Foreign Movement.

General Clayton to Earl Curzon, 8 June 1919, in E. L. Woodward and Rohan Butler (eds),
Documents on British Foreign Policy 1919–1939, first series, Vol. VI (London: HMSO,
1952), pp. 273–4.

DOCUMENT 15 THE IMPERIAL WAR HERO

The American journalist Lowell Thomas helped to make T. E. Lawrence ('Lawrence of Arabia') a national hero and international celebrity after the war. His long-running lecture tour about the desert war included motion picture footage of Lawrence's exploits. Here he waxes eloquently – and misleadingly – about the power Lawrence wielded over the Arabs and the benefits they received from his efforts.

During his seven years' wandering through the desert, dressing like an Arab, living with Arabs in their tents, observing their customs, talking to them in their own dialects, riding on his camel across a broad expanse of lonely country unbroken except by the long purple line of the horizon, lying down at night under a silent dome of stars, Thomas Edward Lawrence drank the cup of Arabian wisdom and absorbed the spirit of the nomad peoples. No Westerner ever acquired greater influence over an Oriental people. He had united the scattered tribes of Arabia and induced chieftains who had been bitter enemies for generations to forget their feuds and fight side by side for the same cause. From remote parts of Arabia swarthy sons of the desert had swarmed to his standard as if he had been a new prophet. Largely by reason of his genius, Feisal and his followers had freed Arabia from Turkish oppression. Lawrence had contributed new life and soul to the movement for Arabian independence. The far-reaching results of his spectacular and successful campaign were destined to play an important part in the final adjustment of Near Eastern affairs. ...

Lowell Thomas, *With Lawrence in Arabia* (first edn, 1924; New York: Popular Library, 1961), p. 222.

DOCUMENT 16   **POST-WAR EMPIRE MIGRATION**

The end of the war released the pent-up flow of emigration from Britain. Social imperialists were determined to ensure this exodus took an imperial turn. Their efforts were coordinated by the Overseas Settlement Committee, whose chairman, Leo Amery, outlines the demographic and economic rationale for state-assisted migration to the empire in this memorandum.

The development of the population and wealth of the whole British Empire is the key to the problem of post-war reconstruction. ... Within certain limits withdrawal of population from the United Kingdom tends to reduce the competition for employment, increase wages, and raise the standard of living; and to such extent as it does this it also tends to increase the birthrate, and so eventually to make good the loss caused by emigration. In so far as those who leave the United Kingdom for settlement in other parts of the Empire achieve success and multiply in their new homes, they tend still further to improve the conditions of employment in the Mother Country and to encourage the growth of its population by providing a growing market for its goods and a continuous supply of necessary foodstuffs and raw materials. In other words a moderate flow of emigration rightly directed tends not only to improve the immediate economic and social conditions in this country, but actually, in the long run, to increase both its total population and man-power.

Leo Amery, Confidential Memorandum, 10 February 1919, pp. 2–3, CO721/3, PRO.

DOCUMENT 17   **THE WEMBLEY EXHIBITION, 1924**

The British Empire Exhibition in Wembley in 1924 promoted the benefits of empire to the British public through trade and informational displays. This excerpt from the exhibition handbook points to the imperialists' belief that the ethnic or 'racial' bonds between the peoples of British stock who inhabited various overseas territories provided the basis for a Greater Britain.

It is safe to say that posterity will regard the British Empire Exhibition of 1924 as having been one of the most significant events in the whole story of our Imperial development. The steady trend of British history has been marked by a long series of accidental and premeditated happenings. Wars, industrial expansion, a growing population, and other vast economic forces have, during the last seventy years, re-shaped the framework of our race. The planting of the flag in many far-flung lands has had the effect of rendering sections of our people remote and self-determinate. Daughter-states have grown into sister-nations, but the various components of Empire have become increasingly interdependent. Wembley will emphasise our racial achievements up to date, and will convey to the visitor not only a wider and more definite idea of what our people have accomplished in the past, but a clearer knowledge of what it will be possible for us to achieve in the future. ... In Queen Victoria's reign people began to grasp the facts that the British Isles needed healthy and fertile lands to which their surplus population might advantageously emigrate, and that our manufacturers needed the raw materials which those lands and emigrants could provide. Within the British Commonwealth of Nations there now exist all the potentialities of manufacture and trade. The Empire is at last on the way towards becoming self-supporting and independent. We need only inter-Empire co-operation to knit together the various powerful communities of consumers and producers within the realm into one great patriotic fabric.

British Empire Exhibition 1924, *Handbook of General Information* (Wembley, 1924),
pp. 3–4.

DOCUMENT 18   ENTERTAINING CONSPIRACIES

John Buchan, a disciple of Lord Milner and propaganda minister during the First World War, became a highly successful author of thriller and adventure tales during the inter-war years. These novels invariably served a didactic purpose, warning against the threat that German spies and other agents of darkness posed to England and its empire. In the following passage from The Thirty-Nine Steps, *the hero preaches the benefits of empire in a public debate against a deluded advocate of socialism and disarmament.*

I never heard anything like it. He didn't begin to know how to talk. ... It was the most appalling rot, too. He talked about the 'German menace', and said it was all a Tory invention to cheat the poor of their rights and keep back the great flood of social reform, but that 'organised labour' realised this and laughed the Tories to scorn. He was all for reducing our Navy as a proof of our good faith, and then sending Germany an ultimatum telling her to do the same or we would knock her into a cocked hat. He said that, but for the Tories, Germany and Britain would be fellow workers in peace and reform. ... I didn't get on so badly when it came to my turn. I simply told them all I could remember about Australia ... – all about its labour party and emigration and universal service. I doubt if I remembered to mention Free Trade, but I said there were no Tories in Australia, only Labour and Liberals. That fetched a cheer, and I woke them up a bit when I started to tell them the kind of glorious business I thought could be made out of the Empire if we really put our backs into it.

John Buchan, *The Thirty-Nine Steps* (first edn, 1926; London: Pan Books, 1959), pp. 52–3.

DOCUMENT 19   INDIRECT RULE

What Frederick Lugard had introduced at the turn of the century in an opportunist effort to secure British control over the newly conquered states of northern Nigeria became by the inter-war era a doctrine of governance that proclaimed its applicability to almost any colonial context. Here Lugard explains how the system worked and what it sought to achieve.

That the principle of ruling through the native chiefs is adopted by the different governments of British Tropical Africa can be seen from recent local pronouncements. ... The object in view is to make each 'Emir' or paramount chief, assisted by his judicial Council, an effective ruler over his own people. He presides over a 'Native Administration' organised through-out as a unit of local government. ... The Resident acts as sympathetic adviser and counsellor to the native chief, being careful not to interfere so as to lower his prestige, or cause him to lose interest in his work. His advice on matters of general policy must be followed, but the native ruler issues his own instructions to his subordinate chiefs and district heads – not as the orders of the Resident but as his own. ... It is the consistent aim of the British staff to maintain and increase the prestige of the native ruler, to encourage his initiative, and to support his authority. That the chiefs are satisfied with the autonomy they enjoy in the matters which really interest and concern them, may be judged by their loyalty and the prosperity of their country.

Sir F. D. Lugard, The Dual Mandate in British Tropical Africa (Edinburgh and London: William Blackwood, 1922), pp. 199–201, 204.

DOCUMENT 20   THE LIMITATIONS OF THE BRITISH LEFT

The frustration that the Indian nationalist leader Jawaharlal Nehru felt towards British leftists shines through in the following passage, where he accuses them of constructing clever rationales for the maintenance of British imperial rule.

We are told that independence is a narrow creed in the modern world, which is increasingly becoming inter-dependent, and therefore in demanding independence we are trying to put the clock back. Liberals and pacifists and even so-called socialists in Britain advance this plea and chide us for our narrow nationalism, and incidentally suggest to us that the way to a fuller national life is through the 'British Commonwealth of Nations'. It is curious how all roads in England – liberalism, pacifism, socialism, etc. – lead to the maintenance of the Empire.

Jawaharlal Nehru, An Autobiography (1st edn, 1936; Delhi: Oxford University Press, 1985), pp. 419–20.

DOCUMENT 21   DIFFERENTIATING DOMINIONS FROM COLONIES

The ethnic bonds and political structures that differentiated the Dominions from the rest of the empire led to a series of initiatives in the 1920s that sought to institutionalise this difference. Leo Amery, then Colonial Secretary, explains to Parliament the decision to create a separate Dominions Office.

The work of the Colonial Office has had to develop progressively on two entirely different lines. There has been, on the one side, the work of communications and consultation between the British Government and its partner Governments over the whole field of their mutual relations and of the common interests of the Empire as a whole. On the other hand, there has been the work of administration and development in that great Colonial area for which this House is directly responsible. These two spheres of work differ, not merely in degree but in kind. The one is political, consultative, and, if I may say so, quasi-diplomatic; the other is administrative and directive. They call for wholly different methods and qualities of mind. It is the consciousness of this difference, and the feeling that it was not always adequately recognised, which, much more than any mere sentimental objection to the word 'Colonial', has always created a certain amount of resentment in the Dominions against the idea that their relations with the Mother Country should be dealt with by the Colonial Office.

Parliamentary Debates, Fifth Series: House of Commons, 1924–25, 187 (London: HMSO, 1925), c. 66.

DOCUMENT 22 MILNER'S IMPERIAL CREDO

Lord Milner was a leading exponent of imperial 'race' patriotism. This 'credo', published shortly after his death, summarizes its main tenets.

CREDO: Key to my position. ... I am a British (indeed primarily an English) Nationalist. If I am also an Imperialist, it is because the destiny of the English race, owing to its insular position and long supremacy at sea, has been to strike fresh roots in distant parts of the world. My patriotism knows no geographical but only racial limits. I am an Imperialist and not a Little Englander because I am a British race patriot. ... It seems unnatural to me – I think it is impossible from my point of view – to lose interest in and attachment to my fellow-countrymen because they settle across the sea. It is not the soil of England, dear as it is to me, which is essential to arouse my patriotism, but the speech, the tradition, the spiritual heritage, the principles, the aspirations of the British race. They do not cease to be *mine* because they are transplanted. My horizon must widen, that is all. I feel myself a citizen of the Empire. I feel that Canada is my country, Australia my country, New Zealand my country, South Africa my country, just as much as Surrey or Yorkshire. ... The wider patriotism is no mere exalted sentiment. It is a practical necessity ... the United Kingdom is no longer the power in the world which it once was, or, in isolation, capable of remaining a power at all. It is no longer even self-supporting. But the British Dominions as a whole are not only self-supporting. They are more nearly self-sufficient than any other political entity in the world. ... This brings us to the first great principle – follow the race. The British State must follow the race. ... Time was in my younger days, when the gradual dissolution of the Empire was regarded as an inevitable, almost a desirable eventuality. This view is no longer anything like so general, anything like so potent as it was. In another 20 years it is reasonable to hope that it may be altogether extinct – that all Britons alike in the Motherland or overseas, will be Imperialists.

Lord Milner, 'Credo', *The Times*, 27 July 1925, p. 13, col. 6.

DOCUMENT 23 **THE OPPOSITION TO COMPROMISE WITH INDIAN NATIONALISTS**

Winston Churchill opposed the government's efforts to negotiate a compromise with Indian nationalists over the future of British rule. Here he explains his objections in a speech to the Indian Empire Society.

What spectacle could be more sorrowful than that of this powerful country casting away with both hands, and up till now almost by general acquiescence, the great inheritance which centuries have gathered? What spectacle could be more strange, more monstrous in its perversity, than to see the Viceroy and the high officials and agents of the Crown in India labouring with all their influence and authority to unite and weave together into a confederacy all the forces adverse and hostile to our rule in India? ... It is a hideous act of self-mutilation, astounding to every nation in the world. The princes, the Europeans, the Moslems, the Depressed classes, the Anglo-Indians – none of them know what to do nor where to turn in the face of their apparent desertion by Great Britain. ... I am against this surrender to Gandhi. I am against these conversations and agreements between Lord Irwin and Mr. Gandhi. Gandhi stands for the expulsion of Britain from India. Gandhi stands for the permanent exclusion of British trade from India. Gandhi stands for the substitution of Brahmin domination for British rule in India. You will not be able to come to terms with Gandhi. You have only to read his latest declarations and compare them with the safeguards for which we are assured the official Conservatives will fight to the end, to see how utterly impossible agreement is.

Winston Churchill, speech on 18 March 1931, reprinted in Joel H. Wiener (ed), *Great Britain: Foreign Policy and the Span of Empire, 1689–1971: A Documentary History*, Vol. IV (New York: Chelsea House, 1972), p. 3039.

DOCUMENT 24   **THE STRATEGIC THREAT POSED BY GERMANY, ITALY AND JAPAN**

The empire played a central role in the strategic considerations of British authorities as they contemplated the prospects of war with the Axis powers. The following passage shows how these considerations lent support to a policy of appeasement.

[I]t will be seen that our Naval, Military and Air Forces, in their present stage of development, are still far from sufficient to meet our defensive commitments, which now extend from Western Europe through the Mediterranean to the Far East. Even to-day we could face without apprehension an emergency either in the Far East or in the Mediterranean, provided that we were free to make preparations in time of peace and to concentrate sufficient strength in one or other of these areas. The lack of a defended Fleet base and dock in the Mediterranean, other than at Malta, is a serious deficiency; the defences and dockyard at Singapore are also uncompleted. So far as Germany is concerned, as our preparations develop, our defence forces will provide a considerable deterrent to aggression. But the outstanding feature of the present situation is the increasing probability that a war started in any one of these three areas may extend to one or both of the other two. Without overlooking the assistance which we should hope to obtain from France, and possibly other allies, we cannot foresee the time when our defence forces will be strong enough to safeguard our territory, trade and vital interests against Germany, Italy and Japan simultaneously. We cannot, therefore, exaggerate the importance, from the point of view of Imperial defence, of any political or international action that can be taken to reduce the number of our potential enemies and to gain the support of potential allies.

Report by the Chiefs of Staff Sub-Committee, Committee of Imperial Defence, 12 November 1937, Secret C. P. 296 (37), CAB 24/273, PRO.

DOCUMENT 25   **THE DOMINIONS AND APPEASEMENT**

The international threats to peace dominated the discussion at the Imperial Conference of 1937. The delegates voiced strong support for the policy of appeasement and tolerance of totalitarian states.

Thus they agreed that for each member of the Commonwealth the first objective is the preservation of peace. In their view the settlement of differences that may arise between nations and the adjustment of national needs should be sought by methods of co-operation, joint enquiry and conciliation. It is in such methods, and not in recourse to the use of force between nation and nation, that the surest guarantee will be found for the improvement of international relations and respect for mutual engagements. ... They noted with interest the statement made ... that Australia would greatly welcome a regional understanding and pact of non-aggression by the countries of the Pacific, and would be prepared to collaborate to that end with all the peoples of the Pacific region in a spirit of understanding and sympathy. They agreed that if such an arrangement could be made it would be a desirable contribution to the cause of peace and to the continued maintenance of friendly relations in the Pacific. ... Finally, the Members of the Conference, while themselves firmly attached to the principles of democracy and to parliamentary forms of government, decided to register their view that differences of political creed should be no obstacle to friendly relations between Governments and countries, and that nothing would be more damaging to the hopes of international appeasement than the division, real or apparent, of the world into opposing groups.

Maurice Ollivier (ed), *The Colonial and Imperial Conferences*, Vol. III, Part 2 (Ottawa: The Queen's Printer, 1954), pp. 436–7.

DOCUMENT 26   COLONIAL DEVELOPMENT AND WAR LOYALTIES

Malcolm MacDonald, Minister of Health, presented the Colonial Development and Welfare Bill to Parliament in May 1940. Although he denies a direct connection between the timing of the legislation and the need to maintain the loyalty of colonial peoples at this moment of crisis, it is clear that he sees the bill as an effort to restore Britain's somewhat tarnished claims to trusteeship. It is also clear that he does not envision any serious alteration of the colonial relationship as a result of the war.

At this critical hour let the world mark the passage of the Colonial Development and Welfare Bill through the British Parliament as a sign of our faith in ultimate victory. This nation will pass triumphantly through its present ordeal. ... When the enemy is worsted and the war is finished, Britain will still exercise vast responsibilities for the government of Colonial peoples. In the meantime we must not default upon our Colonial obligations. ... It seems to me that one of the most notable assurances that our cause is just is the fact that these distant peoples, alien to us in race, who are ruled by us, sprang instantly and spontaneously to our side at the moment of the declaration of war. ... I think it is significant that these 60,000,000 people, scattered over 50 different territories, who are not yet free to govern themselves, who are governed by us, recognise instinctively from that experience that we are the true guardians of the liberties and the happiness of small peoples. Nevertheless, the proposals for assistance towards Colonial development which are contained in this Bill were not devised after the war had begun. They are not a bribe or a reward for the Colonies' support in this supreme crisis. They were conceived long before the war.

Parliamentary Debates, Fifth Series: House of Commons, 1939–40, 361 (London: HMSO, 1940), cc. 41–2.

DOCUMENT 27   **AN EMPIRE RENEWED BY WAR**

While the Second World War put enormous strain on the British Empire, Winston Churchill insisted that it would endure the experience and even emerge from it with a renewed cohesion and purpose.

... [H]ere, amid the wreck of empires, states, nations, and institutions of every kind, we find the British Commonwealth and Empire more strongly united than ever before. In a world of confusion and ruin, the old flag flies. We have not got to consider how to bind ourselves more closely. It would pass the wit of man to do so. It is extraordinary what a poor business it has become to sneer at the British Empire. Those who have tried it in the United States have been discredited. Those who have tried it in the Dominions have found no public backing, although there is free speech for all opinions. Those who decry our Commonwealth of Nations and deride the Mother Country have very little support.

Winston Churchill, speech to House of Commons, 21 April 1944, reprinted in Robert Rhodes James (ed.), *Winston Churchill: The Complete Speeches, 1897–1963*, Vol. VII, 1943–49 (New York: Chelsea House, 1974), p. 6922.

GLOSSARY

Afrikaners   White settlers of mainly Dutch extraction in South Africa; also known as Boers.

Geddes Axe   Harsh budgetary cuts imposed by the government committee chaired by Sir Eric Geddes in 1921.

Gunboat diplomacy   The use of military force to extract economic concessions.

Imperial preference   A system of preferential tariffs intended to encourage trade within empire.

Indian National Congress   The main nationalist organisation in India.

Indirect rule   The use of indigenous authorities for colonial administration.

Informal empire   Economic domination over states and regions that remained politically independent.

Jingoism   Derived from a late nineteenth-century music hall lyric, it refers to chauvinistic enthusiasm by the masses for imperial adventurism.

Lascars   Sailors of Asian or Middle Eastern origin.

Pro-Boer   An epithet applied to British critics of the South African War.

Sinn Fein   The revolutionary nationalist party that directed the Irish war for independence in 1918–21.

Social Darwinism   Derived from Darwinian theory, it provided a pseudo-scientific rationale for imperial conquest and national rivalries as a manifestation of natural selection.

Social imperialism   An effort to create popular support for imperial policies by linking them to social reforms at home.

Sterling area   The economic association of countries and colonies that recognised the British pound sterling as the base currency.

Ulster   A region of Northern Ireland dominated by Protestants who opposed Irish Home Rule.

Unionist   An opponent of Irish Home Rule.

Villa Toryism   A reference to the Tory Party's success among voters in middle-class suburbs in the late nineteenth century.

WHO'S WHO

Amery, Leopold (1873–1955)   One of the most active advocates of the imperial cause on the British political scene. A fervent supporter of Chamberlain's tariff reform campaign and a close associate of Milner, Amery entered Parliament as a Conservative Unionist in 1911. He drafted the Balfour Declaration in 1917, directed the Overseas Settlement Office as Milner's Under-Secretary in the Colonial Office from 1919 to 1921, and served as Colonial Secretary from 1924 to 1929 – and from 1925 concurrently as Dominions Secretary. A critic of appeasement policy, he returned to office in 1940 as Secretary of State for India.

Asquith, Herbert (1852–1928)   Liberal Party leader. He rose to prominence as a member of the Liberal Imperialist wing of the party, supporting the South African War and social imperialism at home. After a successful stint as Chancellor of the Exchequer from 1905 to 1908, he became Prime Minister, piloting his government through a series of controversial issues from the 'people's budget' to Irish Home Rule. Dissatisfaction with his leadership in the First World War led to his ouster in 1916. He never reconciled with his successor, Lloyd George, dividing and marginalising the Liberal Party in the inter-war era.

Chamberlain, Joseph (1836–1914)   'Radical Joe', as his supporters fondly called him, was one of the most charismatic and controversial figures in late-Victorian and Edwardian politics. He began his political career as a reforming mayor of Birmingham in 1873–75, entering Parliament in 1876 and establishing himself as a leader of the radical wing of the Liberal Party. He broke with Gladstone and the Liberal Party over Irish Home Rule in 1886, leading fellow Unionists into an alliance with the Conservatives. He served as a vigorous Colonial Secretary in the Conservative government from 1895 to 1903, but resigned to launch the campaign for tariff reform, with negative repercussions for the Conservatives. He was the most influential advocate of imperialism of his age.

Churchill, Winston (1874–1965)   Scion of the aristocratic Marlborough family and titan of modern British politics. Churchill's early military and journalistic experiences in India, the Sudan and South Africa instilled an enthusiasm for empire that continued over the course of his long career. He entered Parliament as a Conservative MP in 1900, but became a Liberal in 1904 because he objected to Chamberlain's tariff reform campaign. He joined the Liberal Cabinet in 1908, fell from grace after the failure of the Gallipoli campaign in 1915, but returned to favour as Lloyd George's ally, holding several ministerial posts, including Colonial Secretary, until the coalition collapsed in 1922. By 1924 he had returned to the Conservative Party, accepting office as Chancellor of the Exchequer, where he remained until the Labour victory in 1929. He became increasingly estranged from Conservative leaders in the 1930s, objecting to their policies regarding India, Germany, and other matters. With the outbreak of the Second World War, he entered the Cabinet and became Prime Minister in May

1940. An inspirational war leader at home, he pursued a strategy that sought to maintain Britain's imperial might.

Curzon, George, Marquess of Kedleston (1859–1925) Imperial proconsul and war minister. After serving as a Conservative MP from 1886 to 1898 and establishing himself as an authority on Central Asia, he was appointed Viceroy of India in 1898, where his tempestuous term ended prematurely in 1905. He entered the War Cabinet in 1915 and assumed a central role in shaping war imperialism as Foreign Secretary. Although he continued in the subsequent Conservative ministry, his arrogance prevented him from attaining leadership of the party.

Disraeli, Benjamin (1804–81) Founder of the modern Conservative Party and political rival of William Gladstone. As leader of the House of Commons, he was responsible for the passage of the Reform Act of 1867, extending the franchise to most urban male workers. As Prime Minister in 1868 and 1874–80, he was responsible for promoting public pride in the empire, demonstrating the political benefits that could be gained from a policy of imperial expansion.

Gandhi, Mohandas (1869–1948) Leader of the Indian nationalist movement; known as 'the Mahatma' or Great Soul. Trained as a lawyer in London, he began his legal career in Natal, South Africa, where his opposition to pass laws and other racial restrictions laid the groundwork for his innovative efforts against the Raj. He returned to India in 1914 and after the war launched a series of civil disobedience campaigns against British rule, culminating in the 'Quit India' movement in 1942.

Gladstone, William (1809–98) Leader and 'grand old man' of the Liberal Party. He began his political career as a Tory MP, but gravitated to the Liberals after mid-century. He served as Prime Minister in 1868–74, 1880–85, 1886 and 1892–94. A defender of fiscal and religious rectitude, he objected to the imperial policies of Benjamin Disraeli both because of their cost and their disregard for moral considerations. His decision to press for Irish Home Rule in 1886 split his party.

Hobson, John A. (1858–1940) Journalist, economist and critic of imperialism. His opposition to the South African War spurred him to write *Imperialism* (1902), an excoriating critique of imperialism's financial motivations. Though his analysis inspired Marxist interpretations of imperialism, he remained a free trade liberal who placed his faith in the conjunction of a capitalist economy and a democratic state.

Kipling, Rudyard (1865–1936) Nobel Prize-winning author whose work established him as the pre-eminent voice of the British imperial experience. Born in India but educated in England, he began his career as a journalist in India. A collection of his stories about Anglo-Indian society, *Plain Tales From the Hills* (1888), brought him to the attention of the reading public at home. Through a long and highly successful career as the author of novels, short stories, poems and children's tales, he tempered his praise for the virtues of empire with appreciation for its costs.

Kitchener, Horatio (1850–1916) Popular imperial general. He came to fame as commander of the army that crushed the Mahdi's forces in the Sudan in 1898, revenging the death of Gordon. His counter-insurgency strategy against the Afrikaners brought an end to the South African War. He served as Commander-in-Chief of the army in India (1902–9) and Egypt (1911–14), then Secretary of War until his death in 1916.

Law, Andrew Bonar (1858–1923)   Canadian-born Unionist politician. An advocate of imperial preference and defender of the Ulster Protestant community, he led the Conservative campaign against Irish Home Rule in 1914. He held several ministerial posts in the coalition governments of the First World War, including Colonial Secretary, and became Prime Minister following the fall of the Lloyd George coalition in 1922.

Lloyd George, David (1863–1945)   One of the most dynamic figures in twentieth-century British politics. Known by supporters as the 'Welsh wizard', he first came to national notice as a vocal critic of the South African War. As Chancellor of the Exchequer in the pre-war Liberal government, he promoted important social welfare legislation and proposed the 'people's budget' of 1909, which caused outrage among Conservatives. When Asquith proved unequal to the demands of leadership in the First World War, however, Conservatives supported Lloyd George, who formed a coalition government in 1916 that pursued a social imperial agenda at home and imperialist policy abroad. The coalition won a triumphant victory under his leadership in 1918, but frayed under the strain of the early post-war years, coming to an end in 1922. With the Liberal Party divided between Asquith's supporters and his own, Lloyd George never returned to office.

Lugard, Frederick, Baron of Abinger (1858–1945)   Colonial official and theorist. He began his career as an army officer in India, but went to Africa in 1888, spending the next two decades extending the frontiers of British colonial rule in East and West Africa. He was appointed governor of Hong Kong in 1907 and returned to Nigeria as governor in 1912. After retiring from active service in 1919 he argued the case for indirect rule in *The Dual Mandate* (1922), which became the bible of colonial administrators in the inter-war years.

Milner, Alfred, Viscount (1854–1925)   A leading ideologue of the imperialist cause. After an apprenticeship in the colonial administration of Egypt, he was appointed High Commissioner of South Africa in 1897, where he pressed for war and oversaw the post-war reconstruction. He became a prophet to imperial advocates, but a lightning rod for critics. He joined Lloyd George's War Cabinet in 1916 and served as Colonial Secretary from 1918 to 1921.

Morel, E. D. (1873–1924)   Critic of colonial exploitation. He came to prominence for his exposé of the brutal treatment of Africans in the Belgian Congo. Active in leftist politics, he broadened the scope of his concerns to British and other European colonial practices, as well as the effects of secret diplomacy and the Versailles Peace Treaty.

Nehru, Jawaharlal (1889–1964)   Indian nationalist and disciple of Gandhi. Educated at Harrow and Oxford, Nehru entered nationalist politics in 1918 and eventually became second only to Gandhi in his importance to the movement. He negotiated Indian independence in 1946–47.

Rhodes, Cecil (1853–1902)   South African mining magnate and imperial politician. Soon after moving to South Africa for his health in 1870, Rhodes demonstrated a flair for finance, acquiring a controlling interest in the Kimberley diamond mine and investing heavily in the Transvaal gold mines. In 1889 his royal chartered company established claim to the territory north of the Limpopo River, soon known as Southern and Northern Rhodesia. As premier of the Cape Colony from 1890, he struggled against Afrikaner separatism, but went too far with the Jameson Raid, which forced his resignation in 1896. A British 'race' patriot, he preached the creed of imperial expansion and unity.

Salisbury, Robert, 3rd Marquess of (1830–1903) Successor to Benjamin Disraeli as leader of the Conservative Party and architect of late nineteenth-century British foreign policy. He served as Foreign Secretary in 1878–80 and again through most of his tenure as Prime Minister, which encompassed the years 1885–86, 1886–92 and 1895–1902. Salisbury viewed the expansion of the franchise with suspicion, but shepherded the Conservative Party into the age of modern democratic politics; he viewed the international scene with pessimism, but oversaw an unprecedented expansion of the British Empire.

Smuts, Jan (1870–1950) South African and imperial politician. Born into a prominent Afrikaner family but educated at the University of Cambridge, Smuts straddled the fence between Afrikaner nationalist and British imperial interests. He led Afrikaner forces against the British in the South African War, but negotiated self-government for the Transvaal in 1907 and South African unification in 1910. He commanded British imperial forces in the East African campaign in 1916–17, then joined the Imperial War Cabinet in London during the final phase of the war. He served as Prime Minister of South Africa in 1919–24 and again in 1939–48, ensuring his country's involvement in the Second World War. He played a key role in the creation of the British Commonwealth and acquired a reputation in Britain as a great imperial statesman.

Webb, Sidney (1859–1947) and Beatrice (1858–1943) Influential figures in twentieth-century British political and intellectual life. As leaders of the Fabian Society, they advocated a version of state socialism that shared some of the same aims as imperialists like Chamberlain, as evidenced by the short-lived Coefficient Society. Sidney served as Colonial Secretary in the Labour government of 1929–31.

BIBLIOGRAPHY

GUIDE TO FURTHER READING

Students interested in pursuing research on this subject can find a rich array of published material. Perhaps the best single source of information about the influence of imperial issues on the British political consciousness is the *Parliamentary Debates* (HMSO). A treasure trove of documents on British foreign policy can be found in the massive series edited by E. L. Woodward and R. Butler, *Documents on British Foreign Policy 1919–1939* (HMSO). J. H. Wiener (ed.), *Great Britain: Foreign Policy and the Span of Empire, 1689–1971*, 4 vols (New York: Chelsea House, 1972), is a compendious and well-chosen collection, which includes the texts of treaties, speeches, memoranda and other material. A series of volumes edited by F. Madden and J. Darwins draws together important documents in imperial history: those most relevant to our purposes are *The Dominions and India since 1900, Vol. 6* and *The Dependent Empire, 1900–1948, Vol. 7* (Westport, CT: Greenwood, 1993). Also useful is S. R. Ashton and S. E. Stockwell (eds), *Imperial Policy and Colonial Practice, 1925–1945: British Documents on the End of Empire Project*, 2 vols (HMSO, 1996). Another valuable source of primary material is the memoirs, collected speeches and other published writings of influential public figures like Winston Churchill, Joseph Chamberlain and Leo Amery.

The secondary literature on the subjects examined in this survey is voluminous, though most of it tends to focus either on domestic or imperial history rather than the connections between the two. The best introduction to the scholarship on British imperial history is W. R. Louis (editor-in-chief), *The Oxford History of the British Empire*, especially volumes III (*The Nineteenth Century*, edited by A. Porter) and IV (*The Twentieth Century*, edited by J. Brown and W. R. Louis) (Oxford University Press, 1999). These volumes, however, do not give much attention to the impact of the empire on Britain itself. The best survey of British imperialism in this period is B. Porter, *The Lion's Share*, 3rd edn (Longman, 1996). P. J. Cain and A. G. Hopkins, *British Imperialism*, 2 vols (Longman, 1993) is an important study that redirects attention to the metropolitan social and economic engines of empire. Few surveys of British history give much attention to the imperial dimension of the nation's experience, though R. Shannon's *The Crisis of Imperialism 1865–1915* (Paladin Books, 1976) comes closer than most. More characteristic of the neglect of empire is P. Clarke, *Hope and Glory: Britain 1900–1990* (Penguin, 1996), but it is otherwise a lively and informative survey of Britain in the twentieth century.

Most of the scholarship that has sought to reconnect domestic and imperial history has worked along fairly narrow, monographic lines. The most notable exceptions are J. MacKenzie's ambitious and influential study of *Propaganda and Empire* (Manchester University Press, 1984) and D. Cannadine's provocative *Ornamentalism* (New Haven, CT: Yale University Press, 2001). A. Burton has opened up new avenues of enquiry with her books, *Burdens of History* (Chapel Hill,

NC: University of North Carolina Press, 1994) and *At the Heart of the Empire* (Chapel Hill, NC: University of California Press, 1998), as have L. Tabili, '*We Ask for British Justice*' (Ithaca, NY: Cornell University Press, 1994), J. Schneer, *London 1900* (New Haven, CT: Yale University Press, 1999), and others. However, the best study of imperialism's ideological influence on British society and politics remains B. Semmel, *Imperialism and Social Reform* (New York: Anchor Books, 1968). The literature on the relationship between Britain and its empire continues to grow day by day. Although the following references identify the sources that I have drawn on most directly in addressing particular issues in the text, the list of relevant works could easily be doubled or tripled.

REFERENCES

Place of publication is London unless otherwise noted.

Adelson, R. (1995) *London and the Invention of the Middle East: Money, Power, and War, 1902–1922*. New Haven, CT: Yale University Press.

Alford, B. W. (1996) *Britain in the World Economy since 1800*. Longman.

August, T. G. (1985) *The Selling of the Empire: British and French Imperialist Propaganda, 1890–1940*. Westport, CT: Greenwood Press.

Barclay, G. St J. (1976) *The Empire is Marching: A Study of the Military Effort of the British Empire*. Weidenfeld and Nicolson.

Barnett, C. (1972) *The Collapse of British Power*. New York: William Morrow.

Beloff, M. (1970) *Imperial Sunset, Vol. 1: Britain's Liberal Empire, 1897–1921*. New York: Alfred A. Knopf.

Boyce, D. G. (1996) *The Irish Question and British Politics, 1868–1996* (2nd edn). Macmillan.

Brown, J. M. and Louis, W. R. (eds) (1999) *The Oxford History of the British Empire, Vol. IV: The Twentieth Century*. Oxford: Oxford University Press.

Burton, A. (1994) *Burdens of History: British Feminists, Indian Women, and Imperial Culture, 1865–1915*. Chapel Hill, NC: University of North Carolina Press.

Burton, A. (1998) *At the Heart of the Empire: Indians and the Colonial Encounter in Late-Victorian Britain*. Berkeley, CA: University of California Press.

Bush, B. (1999) *Imperialism, Race and Resistance: Africa and Britain 1919–1945*. Routledge.

Bush, J. (2000) *Edwardian Ladies and Imperial Power*. Leicester University Press.

Cain, P. J. and Hopkins, A. G. (1993) *British Imperialism: Vol. 1, Innovation and Expansion 1688–1914; Vol. 2, Crisis and Deconstruction 1914–1990*. Longman.

Callaghan, J. (1997) *Great Power Complex: British Imperialism, International Crises and National Decline, 1914–51*. Pluto Press.

Cannadine, D. (2001) *Ornamentalism: How the British Saw Their Empire*. Oxford: Oxford University Press.

Castle, K. (1996) *Britannia's Children: Reading Colonialism Through Children's Books and Magazines*. Manchester: Manchester University Press.

Chamberlain, M. E. (1974) *The Scramble for Africa*. Longman.

Chanock, M. (1977) *Unconsummated Union: Britain, Rhodesia and South Africa 1900–45*. Manchester: Manchester University Press.

Charmley, J. (1993) *Churchill: The End of Glory*. New York: Harcourt Brace.

Clarke, P. (1996) *Hope and Glory: Britain 1900–1990*. Penguin.

Clayton, A. (1986) *The British Empire as a Superpower, 1919–39*. Macmillan.

Colls, R. and Dodd, P. (eds) (1986) *Englishness: Politics and Culture 1880–1920*. Croom Helm.

Constantine, S. (ed.) (1990) *Emigrants and Empire: British Settlement in the Dominions between the Wars*. Manchester: Manchester University Press.

Coombes, A. E. (1994) *Reinventing Africa: Museums, Material Culture and the Popular Imagination in Late Victorian and Edwardian England*. New Haven, CT: Yale University Press.

Curtis, L. P., Jr (1968) *Anglo-Saxons and Celts: A Study of Anti-Irish Prejudice in Victorian England*. Bridgeport, CT: Conference on British Studies.

Dangerfield, G. (1976) *The Damnable Question: A Study in Anglo-Irish Relations*. Boston, MA: Little, Brown.

Darwin, J. (1986) 'The Fear of Falling: British Politics and Imperial Decline since 1900', *Transactions of the Royal Historical Society*, 5th series, 36: 27–43.

Davin, A. (1978) 'Imperialism and Motherhood', *History Workshop*, 5: 9–65.

Day, D. (1988) *The Great Betrayal: Britain, Australia and the Onset of the Pacific War 1939–42*. New York: W. W. Norton.

Driver, F. (2001) *Geography Militant: Cultures of Exploration and Empire*. Oxford: Blackwell.

Drummond, I. M. (1974) *Imperial Economic Policy 1917–1939*. Toronto, University of Toronto Press.

Eddy, J. and Schreuder, D. (eds) (1988) *The Rise of Colonial Nationalism*. Sydney: Allen and Unwin.

Fedorowich, K. (1995) *Unfit for Heroes: Reconstruction and Soldier Settlement in the Empire between the Wars*. Manchester: Manchester University Press.

Fletcher, I., Mayhall, L. E. N. and Levine, P. (eds) (2000) *Women's Suffrage in the British Empire*. Routledge.

Friedberg, A. L. (1988) *The Weary Titan: Britain and the Experience of Relative Decline, 1895–1905*. Princeton, NJ: Princeton University Press.

Gallagher, J. (1982) *The Decline, Revival and Fall of the British Empire*. Cambridge: Cambridge University Press.

Gupta, P. S. (1975) *Imperialism and the British Labour Movement, 1914–1964*. New York: Holmes and Meier.

Harris, J. (1994) *Private Lives, Public Spirit: Britain 1870–1914*. Penguin.

Havinden, M. and Meredith, D. (1993) *Colonialism and Development: Britain and its Tropical Colonies, 1850–1960*. Routledge.

Headrick, D. R. (1988) *The Tentacles of Progress: Technology Transfer in the Age of Imperialism, 1850–1940*. New York: Oxford University Press.

Heathorn, S. (2000) *For Home, Country, and Race: Constructing Gender, Class, and Englishness in the Elementary School, 1880–1914*. Toronto: University of Toronto Press.

Hetherington, P. (1978) *British Paternalism and Africa 1920–1940*. Frank Cass.

Heussler, R. (1963) *Yesterday's Rulers: The Making of the British Colonial Service*. New York: Syracuse University Press.

Hochschild, A. (1998) *King Leopold's Ghost*. Boston, MA: Houghton Mifflin.

Holland, R. F. (1981) *Britain and the Commonwealth Alliance 1918–1939*. Macmillan.

Holland, R. F. (1991) *The Pursuit of Greatness: Britain and the World Role, 1900–1970.* Fontana Press.

Holmes, C. (1988) *John Bull's Island: Immigration and British Society, 1871–1971.* Macmillan.

Howe, S. (1993) *Anticolonialism in British Politics: The Left and the End of Empire 1918–1964.* Oxford: Clarendon Press.

Huttenback, R. A. (1976) *Racism and Empire: White Settlers and Colored Immigrants in the British Self-Governing Colonies 1830–1910.* Ithaca, NY: Cornell University Press.

Hynes, W. G. (1979) *The Economics of Empire: Britain, Africa and the New Imperialism 1870–95.* Longman.

Jeffery, K. (1984) *The British Army and the Crisis of Empire 1918–1939.* Manchester: Manchester University Press.

Jones, G. (1986) *Social Hygiene in Twentieth Century Britain.* Croom Helm.

Kennedy, D. (1987) *Islands of White: Settler Society and Culture in Kenya and Southern Rhodesia, 1890–1939.* Durham, NC: Duke University Press.

Koebner, R. and Schmidt, H. (1964) *Imperialism: The Story and Significance of a Political Word, 1840–1960.* Cambridge: Cambridge University Press.

Killingray, D. and Rathbone, R. (eds) (1986) *Africa and the Second World War.* Macmillan.

Krozewski, G. (1993) 'Sterling, the "Minor" Territories, and the End of Formal Empire, 1939–1958', *Economic History Review,* 46, 2: 239–65.

Lahiri, S. (2000) *Indians in Britain: Anglo-Indian Encounters, Race and Identity 1880–1930.* Frank Cass.

Le Carré, J. (2000–1) 'The Constant Muse', *The New Yorker,* 25 December–1 January 2001: 66–74.

Levine, P. (1996) 'Rereading the 1890s: Venereal Disease as "Constitutional Crisis" in Britain and British India', *Journal of Asian Studies,* 55, 3: 585–612.

Levine, P. (1998) 'Battle Colors: Race, Sex, and Colonial Soldiery in World War I', *Journal of Women's History,* 9, 4: 104–30.

Lindqvist, S. (1996) *'Exterminate All the Brutes'.* New York: The New Press.

Lloyd, T. O. (1996) *The British Empire 1558–1995* (2nd edn). Oxford: Oxford University Press.

Louis, W. R. (1978) *Imperialism at Bay: The United States and the Decolonization of the British Empire, 1941–1945.* New York: Oxford University Press.

Louis, W. R. (1992) *In the Name of God, Go!: Leo Amery and the British Empire in the Age of Churchill.* New York: W. W. Norton.

Lowe, C. J. (1967) *The Reluctant Imperialists: British Foreign Policy 1878–1902.* Macmillan.

MacKenzie, J. M. (1984) *Propaganda and Empire: The Manipulation of British Public Opinion, 1880–1960.* Manchester: Manchester University Press.

MacKenzie, J. M. (ed.) (1986) *Imperialism and Popular Culture.* Manchester: Manchester University Press.

Mangan, J. A. (1986) *The Games Ethic and Imperialism.* New York: Viking.

Mansergh, N. (1982) *The Commonwealth Experience: Vol. 1, The Durham Report to the Anglo-Irish Treaty; Vol. 2, From British to Multi-Racial Commonwealth* (revised edn). Toronto: University of Toronto Press.

Marks, S. and Trapido, S. (1978) 'Lord Milner and the South African State', *History Workshop,* 8: 50–80.

Marwick, A. (1965) *The Deluge: British Society and the First World War.* New York: W. W. Norton.

Matthew, H. C. G. (1973) *The Liberal Imperialists: The Ideas and Politics of a Post-Gladstonian Elite.* Oxford: Oxford University Press.

Metcalf, T. R. (1994) *Ideologies of the Raj.* Cambridge: Cambridge University Press.

Monroe, E. (1981) *Britain's Moment in the Middle East 1914–71* (new and revised edn). Baltimore, MD: The Johns Hopkins University Press.

Moore, R. J. (1974) *The Crisis of Indian Unity 1917–1940.* Oxford: Clarendon Press.

Munro, J. F. (1984) *Britain in Tropical Africa 1880–1960.* Macmillan.

Nimocks, W. (1968) *Milner's Young Men: The 'Kindergarten' in Edwardian Imperial Affairs.* Durham, NC: Duke University Press.

O'Day, A. (1998) *Irish Home Rule 1867–1921.* Manchester: Manchester University Press.

Orde, A. (1996) *The Eclipse of Great Britain: The United States and British Imperial Decline, 1895–1956.* Macmillan.

Ovendale, R. (1975) *'Appeasement' and the English Speaking World: Britain, the United States, the Dominions, and the Policy of 'Appeasement', 1937–1939.* Cardiff: University of Wales Press.

Page, M. (ed.) (1987) *Africa and the First World War.* New York, St Martin's Press.

Panayi, P. (1994) *Immigration, Ethnicity and Racism in Britain, 1815–1945.* Manchester: Manchester University Press.

Parsons, N. (1998) *King Khama, Emperor Joe, and the Great White Queen: Victorian Britain Through African Eyes.* Chicago, IL: University of Chicago Press.

Penn, A. (1999) *Targeting Schools: Drill, Militarism and Imperialism.* Woburn Press.

Perry, F. W. (1988) *The Commonwealth Armies: Manpower and Organization in Two World Wars.* Manchester: Manchester University Press.

Phillips, A. (1989) *The Enigma of Colonialism: British Policy in West Africa.* James Currey.

Plant, G. F. (1951) *Overseas Settlement: Migration from the United Kingdom to the Dominions.* Oxford: Oxford University Press.

Porter, A. (ed.) (1999) *The Oxford History of the British Empire, Vol. III: The Nineteenth Century.* Oxford: Oxford University Press.

Porter, B. (1968) *Critics of Empire: British Radical Attitudes to Colonialism in Africa 1895–1914.* Macmillan.

Porter, B. (1996) *The Lion's Share: A Short History of British Imperialism 1850–1995* (3rd edn). Longman.

Price, R. (1972) *An Imperial War and the British Working Class.* Routledge.

Reynolds, D. (1991) *Britannia Overruled: British Policy and World Power in the 20th Century.* Longman.

Reynolds, D. (1995) *Rich Relations: The American Occupation of Britain, 1942–1945.* New York: Random House.

Rich, P. B. (1986) *Race and Empire in British Politics.* Cambridge: Cambridge University Press.

Robinson, R. and Gallagher, J. (1953) 'The Imperialism of Free Trade', *Economic History Review*, 6, 1: 1–15.

Robinson, R. and Gallagher, J., with Alice Denny (1968) *Africa and the Victorians: The Climax of Imperialism.* New York: Anchor Books.

Rose, K. (1984) *King George V.* New York: Alfred A. Knopf.

Rose, S. (1998), 'Sex, Citizenship, and the Nation in World War II Britain', *American Historical Review*, 103, 4: 1147–76.

Rosenthal, M. (1986) *The Character Factory: Baden-Powell's Boy Scouts and the Imperatives of Empire.* New York: Pantheon.

Rutherford, J. (1997) *Forever England: Reflections on Masculinity and Empire.* Lawrence and Wishart.

Scally, R. J. (1975) *The Origins of the Lloyd George Coalition: The Politics of Social-Imperialism, 1900–1918.* Princeton, NJ: Princeton University Press.

Schneer, J. (1999) *London 1900: The Imperial Metropolis.* New Haven, CT: Yale University Press.

Searle, G. R. (1971) *The Quest for National Efficiency: A Study of British Politics and Political Thought, 1899–1914.* Berkeley, CA: University of California Press.

Semmel, B. (1968) *Imperialism and Social Reform: English Social-Imperial Thought 1895–1914.* New York: Anchor Books.

Shannon, R. (1976) *The Crisis of Imperialism 1865–1915.* Paladin Books.

Sinha, M. (1995) *Colonial Masculinity: The 'Manly Englishman' and the 'Effeminate Bengali' in the Late Nineteenth Century.* Manchester: Manchester University Press.

Smith, I. R. (1996) *The Origins of the South African War 1899–1902.* Longman.

Spencer, I. (1995) 'World War Two and the Making of Multiracial Britain', in P. Kirkham and D. Thoms (eds), *War Culture: Social Change and Changing Experience in World War Two Britain.* Lawrence and Wishart.

Springhall, J. (1977) *Youth, Empire and Society: British Youth Movements, 1883–1940.* Croom Helm.

Symonds, R. (1991) *Oxford and Empire: The Last Lost Cause?* Oxford: Clarendon Press.

Tabili, L. (1994) *'We Ask for British Justice': Workers and Racial Difference in Late Imperial Britain.* Ithaca, NY: Cornell University Press.

Thompson, A. S. (2000) *Imperial Britain: The Empire in British Politics, c. 1880–1932.* Harlow, Essex: Longman.

Thompson, A. S. (1997) 'The Language of Imperialism and the Meanings of Empire: Imperial Discourse in British Politics, 1895–1914', *Journal of British Studies*, 36: 147–77.

Thorne, C. (1978) *Allies of a Kind: The United States, Britain, and the War against Japan, 1941–1945.* Oxford: Oxford University Press.

Thornton, A. P. (1968) *The Imperial Idea and Its Enemies: A Study in British Power.* New York: Anchor Books.

Tomlinson, B. R. (1979) *The Political Economy of the Raj 1914–1947: The Economics of Decolonization in India.* Macmillan.

Wesseling, H. L. (1996) *Divide and Rule: The Partition of Africa, 1880–1914.* Westport, CT: Praeger.

White, N. J. (1999) *Decolonization: The British Experience since 1945.* Harlow, Essex: Longman.

Wilkinson, R. (1964) *Gentlemanly Power: British Leadership and the Public School Tradition.* Oxford: Oxford University Press.

Williamson, P. (1992) *National Crisis and National Government: British Politics, the Economy and Empire, 1926–1932.* Cambridge: Cambridge University Press.

INDEX

SEMINAR STUDIES IN HISTORY

General Editors: Clive Emsley & Gordon Martel

The series was founded by Patrick Richardson in 1966. Between 1980 and 1996 Roger Lockyer edited the series before handing over to Clive Emsley (Professor of History at the Open University) and Gordon Martel (Professor of International History at the University of Northern British Columbia, Canada and Senior Research Fellow at De Montfort University).

MEDIEVAL ENGLAND

The Pre-Reformation Church in England 1400–1530 (Second edition)
Christopher Harper-Bill   0 582 28989 0

Lancastrians and Yorkists: The Wars of the Roses
David R Cook   0 582 35384 X

Family and Kinship in England 1450–1800
Will Coster   0 582 35717 9

TUDOR ENGLAND

Henry VII (Third edition)
Roger Lockyer & Andrew Thrush   0 582 20912 9

Henry VIII (Second edition)
M D Palmer   0 582 35437 4

Tudor Rebellions (Fourth edition)
Anthony Fletcher & Diarmaid MacCulloch   0 582 28990 4

The Reign of Mary I (Second edition)
Robert Tittler   0 582 06107 5

Early Tudor Parliaments 1485–1558
Michael A R Graves   0 582 03497 3

The English Reformation 1530–1570
W J Sheils   0 582 35398 X

Elizabethan Parliaments 1559–1601 (Second edition)
Michael A R Graves   0 582 29196 8

England and Europe 1485–1603 (Second edition)
Susan Doran   0 582 28991 2

The Church of England 1570–1640
Andrew Foster   0 582 35574 5

STUART BRITAIN

Social Change and Continuity: England 1550–1750 (Second edition)
Barry Coward   0 582 29442 8

James I (Second edition)
S J Houston   0 582 20911 0

The English Civil War 1640–1649
Martyn Bennett   0 582 35392 0

Charles I, 1625–1640
Brian Quintrell   0 582 00354 7

The English Republic 1649–1660 (Second edition)
Toby Barnard   0 582 08003 7

Radical Puritans in England 1550–1660
R J Acheson   0 582 35515 X

The Restoration and the England of Charles II (Second edition)
John Miller   0 582 29223 9

The Glorious Revolution (Second edition)
John Miller   0 582 29222 0

EARLY MODERN EUROPE

The Renaissance (Second edition)
Alison Brown   0 582 30781 3

The Emperor Charles V
Martyn Rady   0 582 35475 7

French Renaissance Monarchy: Francis I and Henry II (Second edition)
Robert Knecht   0 582 28707 3

The Protestant Reformation in Europe
Andrew Johnston   0 582 07020 1

The French Wars of Religion 1559–1598 (Second edition)
Robert Knecht   0 582 28533 X

Phillip II
Geoffrey Woodward   0 582 07232 8

The Thirty Years' War
Peter Limm   0 582 35373 4

Louis XIV
Peter Campbell   0 582 01770 X

Spain in the Seventeenth Century
Graham Darby   0 582 07234 4

Peter the Great
William Marshall   0 582 00355 5

EUROPE 1789–1918

Britain and the French Revolution
Clive Emsley   0 582 36961 4

Revolution and Terror in France 1789–1795 (Second edition)
D G Wright   0 582 00379 2

Napoleon and Europe
D G Wright   0 582 35457 9

The Abolition of Serfdom in Russia, 1762–1907
David Moon   0 582 29486 X

Nineteenth-Century Russia: Opposition to Autocracy
Derek Offord   0 582 35767 5

The Constitutional Monarchy in France 1814–48
Pamela Pilbeam   0 582 31210 8

The 1848 Revolutions (Second edition)
Peter Jones   0 582 06106 7

The Italian Risorgimento
M Clark   0 582 00353 9

Bismarck & Germany 1862–1890 (Second edition)
D G Williamson   0 582 29321 9

Imperial Germany 1890–1918
Ian Porter, Ian Armour and Roger Lockyer   0 582 03496 5

The Dissolution of the Austro-Hungarian Empire 1867–1918 (Second edition)
John W Mason   0 582 29466 5

Second Empire and Commune: France 1848–1871 (Second edition)
William H C Smith   0 582 28705 7

France 1870–1914 (Second edition)
Robert Gildea   0 582 29221 2

The Scramble for Africa (Second edition)
M E Chamberlain   0 582 36881 2

Late Imperial Russia 1890–1917
John F Hutchinson   0 582 32721 0

The First World War
Stuart Robson   0 582 31556 5

Austria, Prussia and Germany, 1806–1871
John Breuilly   0 582 43739 3

EUROPE SINCE 1918

The Russian Revolution (Second edition)
Anthony Wood   0 582 35559 1

Lenin's Revolution: Russia, 1917–1921
David Marples   0 582 31917 X

Stalin and Stalinism (Second edition)
Martin McCauley   0 582 27658 6

The Weimar Republic (Second edition)
John Hiden   0 582 28706 5

The Inter-War Crisis 1919–1939
Richard Overy   0 582 35379 3

Fascism and the Right in Europe, 1919–1945
Martin Blinkhorn   0 582 07021 X

Spain's Civil War (Second edition)
Harry Browne   0 582 28988 2

The Third Reich (Third edition)
D G Williamson   0 582 36883 9

The Origins of the Second World War (Second edition)
R J Overy   0 582 29085 6

The Second World War in Europe
Paul MacKenzie   0 582 32692 3

The French at War, 1934–1944
Nicholas Atkin   0 582 36899 5

Anti-Semitism before the Holocaust
Albert S Lindemann   0 582 36964 9

The Holocaust: The Third Reich and the Jews
David Engel   0 582 32720 2

Germany from Defeat to Partition, 1945–1963
D G Williamson   0 582 29218 2

Britain and Europe since 1945
Alex May   0 582 30778 3

Eastern Europe 1945–1969: From Stalinism to Stagnation
Ben Fowkes   0 582 32693 1

Eastern Europe since 1970
Bülent Gökay   0 582 32858 6

The Khrushchev Era, 1953–1964
Martin McCauley   0 582 27776 0

NINETEENTH-CENTURY BRITAIN

Britain before the Reform Acts: Politics and Society 1815–1832
Eric J Evans   0 582 00265 6

Parliamentary Reform in Britain c. 1770–1918
Eric J Evans   0 582 29467 3

Democracy and Reform 1815–1885
D G Wright   0 582 31400 3

Poverty and Poor Law Reform in Nineteenth-Century Britain, 1834–1914:
From Chadwick to Booth
David Englander   0 582 31554 9

The Birth of Industrial Britain: Economic Change, 1750–1850
Kenneth Morgan   0 582 29833 4

Chartism (Third edition)
Edward Royle   0 582 29080 5

Peel and the Conservative Party 1830–1850
Paul Adelman   0 582 35557 5

Gladstone, Disraeli and later Victorian Politics (Third edition)
Paul Adelman   0 582 29322 7

Britain and Ireland: From Home Rule to Independence
Jeremy Smith   0 582 30193 9

TWENTIETH-CENTURY BRITAIN

The Rise of the Labour Party 1880–1945 (Third edition)
Paul Adelman   0 582 29210 7

The Conservative Party and British Politics 1902–1951
Stuart Ball   0 582 08002 9

The Decline of the Liberal Party 1910–1931 (Second edition)
Paul Adelman   0 582 27733 7

The British Women's Suffrage Campaign 1866–1928
Harold L Smith   0 582 29811 3

War & Society in Britain 1899–1948
Rex Pope   0 582 03531 7

The British Economy since 1914: A Study in Decline?
Rex Pope   0 582 30194 7

Unemployment in Britain between the Wars
Stephen Constantine   0 582 35232 0

The Attlee Governments 1945–1951
Kevin Jefferys   0 582 06105 9

The Conservative Governments 1951–1964
Andrew Boxer   0 582 20913 7

Britain under Thatcher
Anthony Seldon and Daniel Collings   0 582 31714 2

Britain and Empire, 1880–1945
Dane Kennedy   0 582 41493 8

INTERNATIONAL HISTORY

The Eastern Question 1774–1923 (Second edition)
A L Macfie   0 582 29195 X

India 1885–1947: The Unmaking of an Empire
Ian Copland   0 582 38173 8

The Origins of the First World War (Second edition)
Gordon Martel   0 582 28697 2

The United States and the First World War
Jennifer D Keene   0 582 35620 2

Anti-Semitism before the Holocaust
Albert S Lindemann   0 582 36964 9

The Origins of the Cold War, 1941–1949 (Second edition)
Martin McCauley   0 582 27659 4

Russia, America and the Cold War, 1949–1991
Martin McCauley   0 582 27936 4

The Arab–Israeli Conflict
Kirsten E Schulze   0 582 31646 4

The United Nations since 1945: Peacekeeping and the Cold War
Norrie MacQueen   0 582 35673 3

Decolonisation: The British Experience since 1945
Nicholas J White   0 582 29087 2

The Origins of the Vietnam War
Fredrik Logevall   0 582 31918 8

The Vietnam War
Mitchell Hall   0 582 32859 4

WORLD HISTORY

China in Transformation 1900–1949
Colin Mackerras   0 582 31209 4

Japan Faces the World, 1925–1952
Mary L Hanneman   0 582 36898 7

Japan in Transformation, 1952–2000
Jeff Kingston   0 582 41875 5

China since 1949
Linda Benson   0 582 35722 5

US HISTORY

American Abolitionists
Stanley Harrold   0 582 35738 1

The American Civil War, 1861–1865
Reid Mitchell   0 582 31973 0

America in the Progressive Era, 1890–1914
Lewis L Gould   0 582 35671 7

The United States and the First World War
Jennifer D Keene   0 582 35620 2

The Truman Years, 1945–1953
Mark S Byrnes   0 582 32904 3

The Korean War
Steven Hugh Lee   0 582 31988 9

The Origins of the Vietnam War
Fredrik Logevall   0 582 31918 8

The Vietnam War
Mitchell Hall   0 582 32859 4